FOUNDATIONS

of

BRAILLE LITERACY

Evelyn J. Rex, Alan J. Koenig,
Diane P. Wormsley, Robert L. Baker

AFB PRESS

American Foundation for the Blind

Foundations of Braille Literacy

is copyright © 1994 by AFB Press, American Foundation for the Blind, 11 Penn Plaza, New York, NY 10001.

2008 reprint

Printed in the United States of America

Library of Congress Cataloging-in-Publication Data

Foundations of braille literacy / Evelyn J. Rex ... [et al.].
      p.   cm.
    Includes bibliographical references and index.
    ISBN 978-0-89128-934-0 (pbk. : alk. paper)
    1. Blind—Printing and writing systems—United States.   2. Blind
Education—United States. 3. Children, Blind—Education—United
States.   I. Rex, Evelyn J.   II. American Foundation for the Blind.
HV1672.F68 1994   94-32788
411—dc20   CIP

Photo credits: Page 100, Howe Press; page 101, Quantum Technology Pty Ltd; pages 102 and 103, American Printing House for the Blind.

CONTENTS

Foreword   v
Susan J. Spungin and Diane P. Wormsley

Prologue   1

Chapter 1
Perspectives on Literacy   5

Chapter 2
A History of Literacy for People Who Are Blind   15

Chapter 3
Learning Processes of People Who Are Blind   25

Chapter 4
Changing Views on Teaching Reading and Writing   35

Chapter 5
Braille Reading Literacy: Approaches and Strategies   61

Chapter 6
Braille Writing Literacy: Approaches and Strategies   83

Chapter 7
Assessment of Braille Literacy   111

Epilogue   131

Suggested Readings   135

Selected Research   137

Resources   143

Index   149

About the Authors   153

FOREWORD

This book is being published at a time when the concern of the general public over the rate of illiteracy in this country is at an all-time high; when many people are reluctant to pay higher taxes for school and other programs; and when everyone—business, government, and families—seems worried about such issues as vanishing jobs, global competitiveness, the proliferation of information and technology, and the skills needed to support a comfortable life in today's world. Turmoil and change seem to be the order of the day, and people who are blind or visually impaired, along with everybody else, find themselves needing to contend with a multitude of social and economic trends. It is not surprising, then, that braille literacy is on the agenda of every conference within the field of education of children who are blind and visually impaired. All of us may need flexible, up-to-date skills, but existing educational programs for blind and visually impaired children are being eroded—in some cases because of dwindling supplies of teachers, in others because of funding problems—and the reasons are many, the solutions not easy to develop. The publication of *Foundations of Braille Literacy* is therefore remarkably timely.

Nowadays, being able to manage and manipulate information is very important to our success, dignity, and perceived self-worth as individuals. And braille represents information and education—the currency of the future—for blind people. Whatever educational system we have, it is important for us to ensure that blind and visually impaired children have choices in the way they gain access to the information they need. Just as the issues of literacy, high-level skills, and access to information relate to everyone's potential in life, the issue of being literate in regard to braille relates specifically to the life potential of children with visual impairments, whose individual needs may require instruction in various media for reading and writing. *Foundations of Braille Literacy* was intended to contribute to the knowledge available on how to improve braille literacy and provide instruction in braille reading and writing.

There are other reasons why we at the American Foundation for the Blind (AFB) think that this book is both significant and useful. The field of education of people who are blind or visually impaired has always been one in which there is so much to be done that few professionals have the luxury of time to document what works and what does not. This is especially so with respect to the subject of teaching reading and writing using braille. Although the tradition of sharing ideas orally has flourished in settings such as the residential school, where teachers passed on their expertise to those who came after them, most blind and visually impaired children are now educated in settings that do not foster the passing on of information in a nonwritten way.

Today itinerant teachers who travel to various sites provide the bulk of instruction to children who are blind. The teaching of reading and writing depends greatly on the methods used by the school district in which a given child is enrolled. The itinerant teacher must be an expert in all phases of instruction of blind and visually impaired children, of which the teaching of reading and writing is only a part. This book was conceived to help that teacher and others who are called on to provide such instruction to students with visual impairments.

Foundations of Braille Literacy does not describe how to teach reading and writing using braille. A companion volume, *Instructional Strategies for Braille Literacy,* provides that methodology. What it does provide is the background of theory in teaching reading and writing that is currently in use in schools today, as well as information about special considerations in teaching reading and writing using braille. We at AFB hope that this book will be useful to everyone who wishes to advocate for better braille instruction for children who are blind or visually impaired and to anyone who wishes to undertake that instruction effectively.

Susan J. Spungin, Ed.D.
Vice President, National Programs and Initiatives
American Foundation for the Blind

Diane P. Wormsley, Ph.D.
Director, National Initiative on Literacy
American Foundation for the Blind

PROLOGUE

In addressing the need for all Americans to be literate, Newman and Beverstock (1990, p. vi) stated, "Now we are ready as a nation to affirm full literacy as a value that we cannot do without." Individuals who are blind, as well as professionals who provide specialized services and parents of children who are blind, join in this affirmation. The focus on literacy that has permeated our society has had direct effects on the system that serves people who are blind; for example:

- Legislation is being passed throughout the country to require appropriate assessment of and instruction in braille reading and writing.
- Research is being conducted on the needs of adults who are blind and the role that braille plays in the attainment of literacy.
- A national research center on braille literacy has been established at the American Printing House for the Blind.
- Technology is providing people who are blind with immediate access to a wealth of information that was previously much less accessible to them.
- The Americans with Disabilities Act requires that "reasonable accommodations" must be made in public places, so braille and other accessible media are becoming more commonplace.
- Revision and "unification" of the braille codes is under consideration by an international committee with representation from the Braille Authority of North America.

In addition to these direct actions on literacy issues, more subtle influences are being felt as well. People are reexamining their personal beliefs about braille, and a change in attitudes toward braille as a medium for attaining literacy is unfolding. Similarly, professionals who provide services for people who are blind are evaluating their assessment and instructional practices to ensure that all individuals attain full literacy. While change is often unsettling, most consumers and professionals in the field are likely to agree that challenging the status quo has moved professional practices forward in a positive and productive manner.

With this renewed attention to braille literacy, it seems an ideal time to take stock of what we know about braille as a medium for literacy, the ways in which we teach and assess braille reading and writing, and the needs that should be addressed in the future. We hope that this book will provide such a foundation. As with most scholarly writing, a balance must be achieved between theoretical and practical aspects of a particular issue. We believe that a full understanding of an issue such as braille literacy must be solidly grounded in theory, so that our professional practices are based on and guided by a sound body of knowledge.

LITERACY: BASIC ISSUES

We call this book *Foundations of Braille Literacy*. Perhaps the most essential foundation of braille literacy is an understanding of issues and practices in general literacy. Controversies about literacy certainly are not restricted to the field of blindness. Professionals in the area of general literacy are confronting—often with great contention—such issues as how to define *literacy* and the best ways to promote the development of literacy. At the same time, they must address the outcries from the general public over the decline in literacy rates. When one looks at the literature and research in the area of general literacy, two things quickly become apparent. First, the extent of the information available is overwhelming. Books and journal articles on issues and practices in literacy are practically inundating the libraries and bookstores. Second, our understanding of literacy has grown and changed as new research and new conceptual frameworks are introduced.

True to the meaning of "foundation," an understanding of braille literacy must be grounded in a context that provides a broad perspective, both theoretical and practical. At the beginning of each chapter in this book, we present information from the area of general literacy as a basis for subsequent discussion of braille literacy. We hope that this approach will not only provide a broader theoretical basis for the book, but will update the reader on current issues and practices in the area of general literacy as well. As professionals in the field of blindness, we must constantly remind ourselves that our practices in literacy instruction are most effective when based on an understanding of the total context within which braille literacy skills are taught and nurtured. We encourage professionals in the field of blindness to read widely in the area of general literacy (the section in this book on Suggested Readings provides recommendations in this area as well as in literacy and blindness), for a true understanding of braille literacy begins here.

UNIQUENESS OF BRAILLE

Another foundation of braille literacy lies in an understanding of the uniqueness of braille. While the braille and print media share many similarities in literacy, braille literacy has its unique aspects that must be recognized, including:

- Considerations in defining literacy that are unique to persons who are blind.
- Unique perceptual aspects of reading braille.
- Unique ways in which young children who are blind learn language, relate that language to their interaction with braille, and develop an understanding of the purposes of reading and writing.

- Unique features of teaching children who are blind to read and write in braille and assessing their mastery of literacy skills.
- Unique features of using braille literacy skills and other communication strategies to ensure integration into the community and workplace.

We explore these issues and practices throughout most of the book. In addition, the emergence of braille as a universally accepted literacy medium for persons who are blind has its own unique history, beginning even before the story of Louis Braille. This rich history is shared in Chapter 2.

As you read *Foundations of Braille Literacy*, we hope you will take time to reflect on your personal beliefs about braille and your professional practices in fostering the growth of literacy in students or adults with visual impairments. Truly, it is an exciting time to reflect and take action on issues related to the literacy of persons who are blind. Now more than ever, we in the field of blindness are in a position to reexamine current practices and build exemplary literacy programs. It is clear that we must all contribute to this movement in whatever capacity possible, so that the goal of full literacy for all Americans will be realized.

REFERENCES

Newman, A. P., & Beverstock, C. (1990). *Adult literacy: Contexts and challenges.* Newark, DE: International Reading Association.

CHAPTER 1

PERSPECTIVES ON LITERACY

In recent years, the concept of literacy has been expanded from simply the ability to read and write to the ability to communicate meaning through language at various levels of proficiency—from the rudimentary to the highly sophisticated—in a range of educational, social, and cultural contexts. Thus, literacy learning is considered a developmental process that begins at birth and continues throughout life. Indeed, two of the six national education goals stated in former President Bush's *America 2000: An Education Strategy* (1991, p. 3) reflect this view:

Goal 1: All children in America will start school ready to learn.

Goal 5: Every adult American will be literate and will possess the knowledge and skills necessary to compete in a global economy and exercise the rights and responsibilities of citizenship.

This chapter presents several perspectives on literacy as a developmental and integrated language-communication process and describes the different forms of literacy: developmental literacy, social literacy, cultural literacy, and knowledge-based literacy. It points out that children who are blind have as much of a right to attain higher and higher levels of literacy as do children with normal vision and that braille is the primary medium that can help them continuously grow in literacy. The information in this chapter serves as background for the remaining chapters, which focus specifically on teaching reading and writing to children who are blind or visually impaired.

LITERACY: AN INTEGRATED LANGUAGE-COMMUNICATION PROCESS

The current view of reading and writing as integrated language processes stresses that reading and writing are two interrelated components of language development and are not discrete skills to be taught in isolation (see Figure 1-1).

5

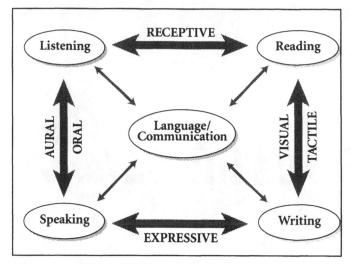

Figure 1-1. Integrated Language-Communication Model.
Source: "Implementing Holistic Literacy Strategies in Chinese Teacher Preparation Programs," by R. Baker and M. Shaw-Baker, paper presented at the International Reading Association 14th World Congress on Reading, Maui, HI, July 1992.

Fundamental to all aspects of language development is the basic need or desire to communicate through language, whether by expressing (encoding) meaning through speaking and writing, or by receiving (decoding) meaning through listening and reading. In either case, meaningful communication involves ongoing interactions between the speaker and listener (oral–aural language) and between the reader and writer (visual or tactual language.)

Most authorities agree that children who enter school with well-developed listening and speaking language skills find it easier to learn to read and write. It has been estimated that the average 6 year old enters school with an oral meaning vocabulary of 6,000 words and has already mastered 90 to 95 percent of basic English syntax (Norton, 1989).

For nearly 30 years, advocates of the language experience approach have supported the view that children should be taught to read words, sentences, and stories that they dictate to teachers on the basis of their own oral language and real-life experiences. Van Allen's (1976) summation of language experience theory as reported by Vacca, Vacca, and Gove (1991, p. 41) simply states: "What I think about, I can talk about; what I can say, I can write or someone can write for me; what I can write, I can read; and I can read what other people write for me to read."

Proponents of other holistic language theories, notably "whole language" theory, have suggested that children should be taught to read and write in the same natural way that they developed their oral language abilities before they entered school and have stressed the inter-relationship between reading and writing (Goodman, 1976). Although debates between advocates of holistic language theories and of more basic skills-oriented theories of teaching reading and writing continue, educators now agree that reading, writing, listening, and speaking are components of integrated language processes, not isolated components of language.

LITERACY'S EXPANDING CONCEPTUAL FRAMEWORK

Figure 1-2 illustrates some of the many educational, social, and cultural applications in the expanded conceptual framework of literacy. Basic to each type of literacy described is the ability to communicate meaning through written language.

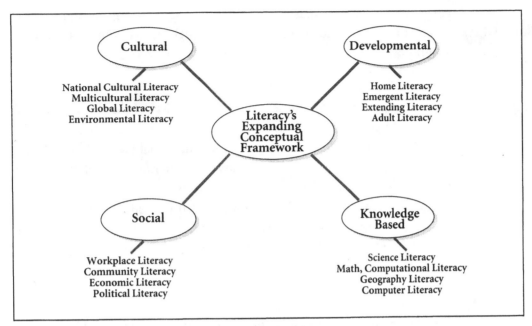

Figure 1-2. The Expanded Conceptual Framework of Literacy

Developmental Literacy

The previously stated view of literacy as a lifelong developmental process is basic to an understanding of literacy learning. As Anderson, Hiebert, Scott, and Wilkinson (1985, p.16) noted, "reading, like playing a musical instrument, is not something that is mastered once and for all at a certain age. Rather, it is a skill that continues to improve through practice." The same can be said for writing, speaking, and listening.

Furthermore, current developmental views of literacy represent a dramatic change from past deficit views of literacy. The previous models focused on deficit views involving illiteracy (the inability to read or write), aliteracy (having the ability to read and write, but choosing not to), and even adult literacy, which often indicated the need for various degrees of "catch-up," remedial instruction. In contrast, developmental views recognize that reading (language) ability develops over time and that readers read differently at different stages in their development (Leu & Kinzer, 1991).

The increased use of terms such as *preschool home literacy, emergent literacy, extending literacy,* and *adult literacy* represents broad stages on the continuum of developmental literacy. Basic to these or any other stages along the continuum are developmental language abilities and cumulative real-life and school-related experiences.

Knowledge-Based Literacy

The ability to read and write implies the need to communicate meaningful, knowledge-based information. Over 20 years ago, Herber (1970) stated that effective language instruction involves teaching both content (subject matter) and process (reading) simultaneously. More recently, *America 2000: An Education Strategy* (1991) emphasized the expanded knowledge-based context of literacy learning in its proposal that all American students should be competent in "English, mathematics, science, history, and geography."

Social Literacy

Literacy education extends beyond formal schooling into a variety of social contexts—the home, the workplace, the community, the marketplace, and the voting booth, among others. Newman and Beverstock (1990, p. 41) suggested that functional literacy is a multifaceted social concept—that is, literacy implies the ability to function well at real-world tasks rather than on school-based, standardized reading assignments.

"Functioning well at real-world tasks" suggests the need for collaborative efforts by school and community agencies. From a social point of view, the role of "teacher" in the present decade and beyond is expanding to include parents, employers, social agencies, volunteers, penal institutions, and the armed services.

Cultural Literacy

Hirsch (1987) reinforced the concept that language communication and thinking depend on a common knowledge base about American culture—its history, literature, language bases, fine arts, sciences, geography, economy, and politics. His concept of cultural literacy extends to multicultural literacy concepts, both domestically and internationally. *America 2000* (1991) expanded this notion to include the importance of global literacy knowledge and skills that are necessary "to compete in a global economy."

LITERACY: LEVELS OF PROFICIENCY

Mason and Au (1990) stated that unlike people in developing countries, individuals in developed countries, such as the United States, need high levels of literacy to take full advantage of social and economic opportunities. They cited the following five levels of literacy, described in the U.S. National Assessment of Educational Progress (NAEP)(Mason & Au, pp. 2-3):

1. Rudimentary: Able to carry out simple reading tasks, such as following brief written directions or selecting the phrase to describe a picture.
2. Basic: Able to understand specific or sequentially presented information, such as locating facts in uncomplicated stories and news articles.
3. Intermediate: Able to see the relationships among ideas and to generalize, such as making generalizations about main ideas and the author's purpose.
4. Adept: Able to understand, summarize, and explain complicated information, such as analyzing unfamiliar material and providing reactions to whole texts.
5. Advanced: Able to synthesize and learn from specialized reading materials, such as extending and restructuring ideas in scientific articles or literary essays.

VIEWS OF LITERACY FOR PERSONS WHO ARE BLIND

An Integrated View of Literacy

Professionals who work with individuals who are blind have always viewed literacy as an integrated process involving reading, writing, speaking, and listening—which have been called "communication skills"—and have realized that all these skills must be developed to their maximum and be integrated meaningfully with life skills. Curry and Hatlen (1988) identified communication skills as a part of the "unique" curriculum for students who are blind or visually impaired, a view that has received widespread endorsement. However, only recently have all aspects of communication been referred to as literacy.

Although reading and writing are the primary literacy skills by conventional definition, speaking and listening are ways to obtain information that is not presented in braille. For example, a person who is blind may gain access to a national newspaper through a telecommunications system by entering appropriate commands on a microcomputer (a writing skill). Then he or she may review the contents of the newspaper aurally using a speech synthesis device (a listening skill) and select pertinent articles to be translated and printed in braille for more careful examination (a reading skill). However, if the telecommunications system is undergoing technical difficulties at the time, the person may request and direct (a speaking skill) that a live reader review the paper aloud (a listening skill). Regardless of the combination of communication skills used, this person independently gained access to and made meaningful use of information in the newspaper. All would likely agree that this individual demonstrated literacy.

Dimensions of Literacy

As the concept of literacy is expanded to encompass more and more aspects of daily life, it is increasingly difficult to gain a consensus on the definition of literacy. Indeed, the framework presented previously indicates that a single definition of literacy may be insufficient to encompass all aspects of this construct. It is clear, however, that educators no longer support a sharp dichotomy between literacy and illiteracy (Venezky, Wagner, & Ciliberti, 1990). The NAEP definition of literacy presented earlier suggests that there are levels or degrees of literacy, a notion that is widely accepted today. Despite acceptance of the notion that literacy is a multifaceted construct, however, there is still no common definition or framework. In an attempt to develop such a framework for understanding the literacy of persons who are blind, Koenig (1992) examined a range of definitions of literacy and synthesized the common characteristics of three levels of literacy: emergent literacy, basic literacy, and functional literacy.

Emergent Literacy

Emergent literacy includes early interactions with written language—for example, scribbling, telling stories from pictures, and recognizing logos of favorite restaurants—that young children with normal vision generally engage in. Such experiences with written language are not readily accessible to children who are blind. As Swenson (1988, p. 336) noted:

> Blind children certainly do not come to school with the same repertoire of literacy behaviors as sighted children. Their lack of exposure to the wealth of written language that surrounds every sighted child, and the relative scarcity of preschool braille materials, may mean that they do not even have the basic concept that spoken language can be written down.

To overcome the lack of incidental exposure to written materials, teachers of students who are blind and family members must work as a team to provide direct, repeated, and meaningful interactions with braille literacy materials and events to children beginning in infancy. Activities suggested by Miller (1985) that can become a natural part of home life for young children who are blind are outlined in "Activities that Promote Emergent Literacy in Young Children Who Are Blind" on the next page.

Basic Literacy

Basic literacy, sometimes called academic literacy, is the kind of reading and writing that occurs in school: reading textbooks and literature, writing essays, taking tests, and taking notes from an encyclopedia or a chalkboard. Students who are blind will develop basic literacy skills in their main literacy medium—braille. During the primary school years, students need intensive and high-quality instruction in literacy by a professional who is knowledgeable about braille and about teaching reading and writing in braille to attain an adequate level of basic literacy skills. The amount of time spent in teaching basic literacy in the regular classroom can serve as a guide to the time needed to teach basic braille literacy skills. Establishing basic literacy skills is a major focus of the early curriculum in primary school, and regular classroom teachers of young children devote a substantial portion of the school day to it. Typically, instruction in reading, writing, spelling, and English (the "language arts") takes 1½ to 2 hours each day, and teachers who espouse a holistic approach to teaching literacy believe that the entire school day is devoted to literacy instruction.

For young children who are blind, the special educator needs at least the same amount of time—1½ to 2 hours per day—for specialized instruction in braille reading and writing. Although it defies logic to assume that braille reading and writing instruction would take *less* time than teaching basic literacy in a regular classroom, one could argue that *additional* instructional time is required to teach special skills. In addition to the time devoted to direct instruction of literacy skills in braille, time is spent consulting with the regular classroom teacher, co-teaching or demonstration teaching in the regular classroom, preparing materials, and so forth. As children complete the later primary grades and go on to junior high school, the focus of special instructional time will shift from teaching basic literacy skills to specific applications of literacy (or functional literacy, as discussed in the next section).

ACTIVITIES THAT PROMOTE EMERGENT LITERACY IN YOUNG CHILDREN WHO ARE BLIND

- Provide a variety of tactual books for the child to explore.

- Read from "twin vision" books that contain both print and braille.

- Adapt print books by placing braille above or below the lines of print.

- Adapt book covers to make them meaningful, perhaps by gluing on an object from the story.

- Make "book bags" that contain objects from the story. While reading aloud, let the child explore the objects that go with the various parts of the story.

- After reading aloud, act out stories with the child.

- Let the child scribble with a braillewriter, after or in conjunction with repeated modeling of the use of braille writing equipment.

- Let the child use a raised-line drawing kit for drawing and scribbling.

- While the child dictates, write stories in braille about the child's experiences or keep a journal; then read these stories together.

- Make an "auditory experience album" by recording events and experiences on cassette tapes; review the album occasionally as you would a book or picture album.

- While reading predictable stories, leave off the ends of sentences and let the child finish them.

- Have the child practice tracking in real braille books while you read aloud; when the child stops tracking, you stop reading.

- Work with the child on the prerequisites to reading and book behavior: moving left to right, turning pages, and recognizing the top and bottom of pages, for example.

Source: Based on "Reading Comes Naturally: A Mother and Her Blind Child's Experiences," by D. D. Miller, 1985, *Journal of Visual Impairment & Blindness, 79*, pp. 1-4.

Regardless of the service delivery model, students who are blind need access to specialized instruction on a consistent and ongoing basis to develop basic literacy. In some instances, however, the movement toward integration and full inclusion has prevented some students from receiving specialized instruction in reading and writing braille. This situation is unconscionable because it is clear that children who are blind need specialized instruction to develop special skills.

One has only to examine the range of literacy tasks that adults perform daily to know that basic or academic literacy is only part of the total literacy continuum. For example, the ability to read and appreciate a fable by Aesop does not directly prepare one to read a bus schedule, nor does writing a term paper prepare one to complete a job application. Obviously, there is a dimension of literacy that relates to the more practical, daily literacy tasks that permeate the lives of people in our society. This dimension is typically referred to as functional literacy.

Functional Literacy

A number of factors characterize functional literacy for persons who are blind. First, the individual demonstrates skills in performing a wide range of literacy tasks that are required in his or her daily life. The specific tasks depend on the individual's specific needs, especially in the workplace. Table 1-1 presents some typical literacy tasks, most of which are functional tasks, that are performed at home, in school, in the community, and at work.

Second, persons who are blind must address the audience for which specific literacy tasks are intended. When the audience for a literacy task is oneself, one is both the reader and writer and, therefore, can choose the medium in which the task will be completed since the information is for personal use only. However, when a task involves communication with others, one is either the reader *or* the writer, but not both. Therefore, unless a person who is blind is communicating with another person who is literate in braille, he

Table 1-1. Functional Literacy Tasks in Four Environments

Audience	Home	School	Community	Work
Communicating with self*	Labeling personal items	Jotting assignments	Making shopping lists	Jotting notes to self
	Maintaining an address and telephone book	Taking notes in class	Writing directions to a specific location	Making lists of "things to do"
Communicating with others**	Writing personal letters to friends	Reading textbooks and workbooks	Completing deposit slips at a bank	Reading memos from supervisor
	Paying bills	Reading periodicals	Reading signs	Writing reports
	Reading mail	Writing term papers	Reading menus	Reading gauges and dials
	Reading for pleasure	Completing assignments	Signing documents	Filling out forms
	Reading newspapers	Taking tests	Writing checks at a store	Reading job manuals
	Reading books to others	Completing registration forms	Reading labels on items at store	Writing work-related correspondence

Source: "A Framework for Understanding the Literacy of Individuals with Visual Impairments," by A. J. Koenig, *Journal of Visual Impairment & Blindness*, 86, p. 279. Copyright © 1992 American Foundation for the Blind. Reprinted by permission.

*The individual is both the writer and the intended reader.
**The individual is either the writer or the intended reader, but not both.

or she will choose to write in print, since it is the most commonly used medium for reading and writing.

Third, persons who are blind must use appropriate tools for gaining access to print independently, when necessary. Some possible tools are recorded media, a typewriter, the assistance of a sighted reader, a radio reading service, print as a supplement to braille, and accessible technology. Independently gaining access to print is often necessary when literacy tasks require communication with others.

The task of educators and rehabilitation specialists is to provide ample opportunities for persons who are blind to master the functional literacy tasks they need for living fully; to use strategies to gain access to print independently, when necessary; to continue to learn new strategies and skills after they leave an instructional program; and to demonstrate self-advocacy skills for gaining information. As Koenig (1992, p. 282) noted, "with self-advocacy skills and a philosophy of ongoing learning, the individual is empowered to challenge and accomplish all functional literacy tasks, regardless of whether he or she has encountered such tasks before."

Literacy is truly a dynamic and multifaceted construct. Despite continuing attempts to define the term, there is still a wide range of opinions of what it does and does not include. Whatever strides the field takes to define the various components or aspects of literacy for persons who are blind, it must do so in the context of the more global efforts that are taking place in general literacy. Moreover, although such a definition or framework must be consistent with the trends in general literacy, it must also consider and give attention to the unique aspects of literacy for persons who are blind.

SUMMARY

This chapter has provided a brief overview of the expanding dimensions of literacy. It suggested that literacy learning is a

- language-based process
- meaning-centered process
- developmental process
- knowledge-based process
- social process
- cultural process

The learning processes are essentially the same for persons who are blind and for sighted persons, but educators must address additional and unique facets of literacy when teaching people who are blind.

Young children who are blind need direct exposure to, and experiences with, literacy activities that are generally gained incidentally by children with normal vision. Students who learn reading and writing in braille during the formal school years need consistent and intense interactions with teachers who will provide high-quality, specialized instruction. Furthermore, all individuals who are blind must acquire specialized skills to perform real-life literacy tasks that they need to live, learn, and work on a daily basis, and they need strategies to gain access to print independently, when necessary. This holistic and specialized view of literacy instruction prepares persons who are blind to function and contribute in a society that is immersed in print, where full integration is dependent on literacy.

REFERENCES

America 2000: An education strategy (1991). Washington, DC: U.S. Department of Education.

Anderson, R. C., Hiebert, E. H., Scott, J. A., & Wilkinson, I. A. G. (1985). *Becoming a nation of readers: The report of the Commission on Reading.* Washington, DC: National Academy of Education, National Institute of Education.

Curry, S. A., & Hatlen, P. H. (1988). Meeting the unique educational needs of visually impaired pupils through appropriate placement. *Journal of Visual Impairment & Blindness, 82,* 417-424.

Goodman, K. (1976). Reading: A psycholinguistic guessing game. In H. Singer & R. Ruddell (Eds.), *Theoretical models and processes of reading* (2nd ed.). Newark, DE: International Reading Association.

Herber, H. L. (1970). *Teaching reading in content areas.* Englewood Cliffs, NJ: Prentice-Hall.

Hirsch, E. D. (1987). *Cultural literacy: What every American needs to know.* Boston: Houghton Mifflin.

Koenig, A. J. (1992). A framework for understanding the literacy of individuals with visual impairments. *Journal of Visual Impairment & Blindness, 86,* 277–284.

Leu, D. J., & Kinzer, C. K. (1991). *Effective reading instruction, K-8* (2nd ed.). New York: Merrill.

Mason, J. M., & Au, K. H. (1990). *Reading instruction for today.* Glenview, IL: Scott, Foresman.

Miller, D. D. (1985). Reading comes naturally: A mother and her blind child's experiences. *Journal of Visual Impairment & Blindness, 79,* 1-4.

Newman, A. P., & Beverstock, C. (1990). *Adult literacy: Contexts and challenges.* Newark, DE: International Reading Association.

Norton, D. A. (1989). *The effective teaching of language arts* (3rd ed.). Columbus, OH: Merrill.

Swenson, A. M. (1988). Using an integrated literacy curriculum with beginning braille readers. *Journal of Visual Impairment & Blindness, 82,* 336–338.

Vacca, J. L., Vacca, R. T., & Gove, M. K. (1991). *Reading and learning to read* (2nd ed.). Boston: Little, Brown.

Van Allen, R. (1976). *Language experiences in education.* Boston: Houghton Mifflin.

Venezky, R. L., Wagner, D. A., & Ciliberti, B. S. (Eds.) (1990). *Toward defining literacy.* Newark, DE: International Reading Association.

A HISTORY OF LITERACY
FOR PEOPLE WHO ARE BLIND

The rank and file of finger readers had a good deal of sympathy with a speaker at one of the national conventions who in a burst of oratory said, "If anyone invents a new system of printing for the blind, shoot him on the spot."   Irwin (1955/1970, p. 47)

Until braille was developed in the early 1800s by Louis Braille, a young student at L'Institute Nationale des Jeunes Aveugles in Paris, there was no effective way for people who were blind or visually impaired to become literate. This chapter presents a brief history of the attainment of literacy by blind people. It clearly demonstrates the enormous impact that the invention of braille had on the literacy of blind people and describes the evolution of the braille code to its current forms.

LITERACY IN EARLY SOCIETIES

Literacy is generally tied to a specific language; someone who is literate in English, for instance, may not be literate in French or Thai. Literacy requires not only an understanding of a language, but the ability to read and write it. Written language, upon which literacy depends, most likely developed when oral communication was no longer sufficient for conveying information about a society's history and traditions from one generation to the next or about the current day-to-day activities of that society, probably because the information that people needed was too complex to be remembered (Gaur, 1992, p. 14). The symbols that made up written language differed from society to society, but the purpose remained the same: to record information that should not be forgotten.

In many early societies, only the privileged classes were permitted to read and write, and the written forms of language were used primarily for religious and mercantile purposes. Moreover, written symbols sometimes had several levels of meanings, the highest of which were, again, learned only by the higher classes. For example, in 10th century Japan, women

15

were allowed to use only the Japanese characters and the phonetic script, while "the Chinese language and the Chinese script—which were considered more prestigious—remained the exclusive and highly prestigious medium for any serious writing among men" (Gaur, 1992, p. 161). In these early societies, the symbols used to convey language were visual and two-dimensional, with just a few exceptions, such as the quipus (knotted cords) used by the Incas of Peru (Gaur, 1992). The use of visual symbols meant that in every society, people who were blind or visually impaired were excluded from becoming literate.

However, in these early societies, literacy was the least concern for people who were blind or visually impaired. Because the inability to see aroused two emotions in people—fear and sympathy—people who were blind or visually impaired were either persecuted or considered useless and hence were kept in abject poverty and ignorance. As French (1932, p. 41) stated:

> Doubtless blindness was looked upon as the worst evil that could befall man, and often as a punishment. Though certain blind persons attained a sort of spiritual preeminence, inspiring even a superstitious awe, the great mass was looked upon as practically useless, and some were at times given over for destruction. While feelings of humanity afforded some a tolerable existence, the majority led the wretched life of beggars. No one had thought of systematically educating them for useful employment.

Among those people who were blind who gained historical prominence were Homer, Didymus, St. Herve, Prince Hitoyasu, Abdu'l Ala Al Ma'arri, Prospero Fagnani, John Milton, Nicholas Saunderson, John Metcalf, Francois Huber, Melanie de Salignac, and Maria Theresa von Paradis (Farrell, 1956). Many prominent blind or visually impaired persons were bards—musicians and poets who traveled from place to place singing songs and recounting folklore. Ironically, the invention of printing and the development of easier modes of travel lessened the need for the oral tradition and "doomed this way of life for the blind bards, for people lost interest in their entertainment and their lore" (Farrell, p. 5).

EARLY LEADERS IN EDUCATION

It was not until the 18th century that people who were blind were considered capable and worthy of being educated. This change in attitude was the result of the work of three Frenchmen: Denis Diderot and Valentin Haüy in the 18th century and Louis Braille in the early 19th century.

Diderot

In 1749, Diderot, a philosopher and editor of the monumental *L'Encyclopédie*, published "Letter on the Blind for the Use of Those Who See," which expressed his beliefs about blindness and the results of his interviews with people who were blind. In a subsequent edition of the letter in 1760, he described the accomplishments of Melanie de Salignac, a woman who was blind and was taught to read by the use of cutout letters and to write by pricking letters onto a piece of paper held in place on a frame. This document had one important consequence: It planted the idea that people who were blind were capable of being educated and that their intellectual abilities were intact, despite their loss or lack of vision (Farrell, 1956).

Haüy

It took more than Diderot's letters, however, to create the attitude toward education of people who are blind that exists today. The abilities of a handful of obviously privileged people who were blind did not immediately convince society that all people who were blind could be educated. It took the efforts of Valentin Haüy, a Frenchman who worked as a translator for the Ministry of Foreign Affairs in Paris.

In 1771, Haüy observed a group of blind musicians in a caricature of themselves that he did not find amusing and resolved to do something to help people who were blind (Farrell, 1956; French, 1932). His meeting in 1780 with Maria Theresa von Paradis, a "cultured blind baroness of Austria, a composer and skilled organist" who performed in Paris (Rodenberg, 1955, p. 3), convinced him to perform an experiment to educate a blind pupil. That experiment, conducted in 1784 with a young beggar who was blind, Francois Lesueur, led to the formation of L'Institute Nationale des Jeunes Aveugles in Paris, the first of many schools for children who were blind that were founded in Europe and England in the 18th century. It was at this school that Haüy invented raised letters that were used as a reading medium for people who were blind. Although the raised letters proved less effective than Haüy had hoped, their invention opened the door to the promotion of the sense of touch as the means by which people who were blind would become literate. The next step was to find the best way to present information to that sense.

Braille

Many efforts were made to develop a style of type that would create letters that could be felt easily and accurately by the fingers. The real breakthrough was the invention of the raised-dot code. Charles Barbier, a cavalry officer attached to the French signal corps, developed a code based on a 12-dot cell (see Figure 2-1) as a means of "night writing" that "would be meaningless to the enemy and could be employed in darkness" (Farrell, 1956, p. 97). This system somehow found its way to Paris to the school for children who were blind, where it was dismissed by the director. In 1829, Louis Braille, a 15-year-old pupil at the school, began to play with the system and adapted it into the six-dot cell system. He and the other pupils, who before then could neither read nor write, used it informally to communicate with each other and take notes in class.

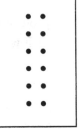

Figure 2-1. Barbier's Cell

By 1834, when he published *Method of Writing Words, Music and Plain Songs by Means of Dots, for Use by the Blind and Arranged for Them*, Braille had most of the details of the code in place. It was not until the early 1900s, however, that the braille code was accepted in the United States as the medium for reading and writing by people who are blind.

BATTLE OF THE TYPES

During the nearly 100 years between the development and acceptance of the braille code in this country, there were many experiments with various type styles of raised-print letters in an attempt to find the "best" type for people to read by. Only one of the many forms has survived. Moon type, originated by Dr. William Moon (Illingworth, 1910), took the Roman capital letters and reduced them to their simplest form or created new characters when he could not modify them (see Figure 2-2). Books were printed to be read in alternating directions from one line to the next. Books in Moon are still used, particularly in Europe with people who have lost their eyesight when they are elderly. The Fishburne alphabet (see Figure 2-3), which was developed more recently, is also used with elderly people who cannot or do not wish to learn braille (Newman & Hall, 1988; Shafrath, 1986).

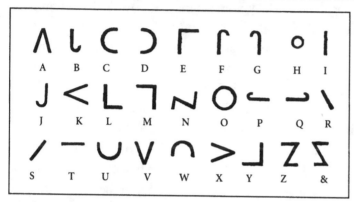

Figure 2-2. Moon Type

This was one of the most frustrating eras in the history of literacy for people who are blind, often referred to as the battle of the types or the "war of the dots" (Irwin 1955/1970). Many educators were hesitant to let go of the raised-print type faces, believing that blind people should be able to communicate in the same code as people with normal vision. However, people who were blind were more comfortable with braille because it was easy for them to use. Initially, braille was officially prohibited at L'Institute des Jeunes Aveugles, but the students and professors who were blind used it surreptitiously. It was not officially adopted by the school until 1854, two years after Braille's death—and then only at the insistence of those who had been using the system (Farrell, 1956).

Braille was slow to expand beyond the school in Paris, but eventually reached England and the United States, where it had to compete with Boston line type developed by Samuel Gridley Howe, as well as with other dot or point codes. The various alternatives to braille that appeared before 1932 attracted their own advocates and

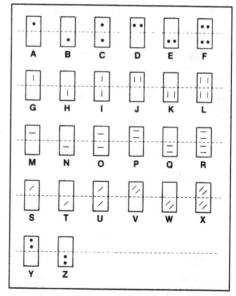

Figure 2-3. The Fishburne Alphabet.
Source: "Ease of Learning the Braille and Fishburne Alphabets," by S. E. Newman and A. D. Hall, *Journal of Visual Impairment & Blindness, 82,* p. 148. Copyright © 1988, American Foundation for the Blind. Reprinted by permission.

Figure 2-4. New York Point

Capital Letters

A	B	C	D	E	F
G	H	I	J	K	L
M	N	O	P	Q	R
S	T	U	V	W	X
Y	Z

Lower-Case Letters

a	b	c	d	e	f	g	h	i	j
k	l	m	n	o	p	q	r	s	t
u	v	w	x	y	z

Figure 2-4. New York Point

created dissension among the proponents of education of blind people. The more powerful competitors were New York Point, American braille, and British braille, grades 1 and 2 (see Figures 2-4 and 2-5) (Illingworth, 1910). They differed from one another with respect to the number of dots per cell, the orientation of the dots (horizontal versus vertical), and the meaning assigned to the various cells. British braille and modified American braille kept the six-dot (two wide and three high) configuration that Braille had devised. New York Point, developed at the New York Institute for the Blind, used cells that were two dots high but expandable horizontally to four dots wide. British braille kept the alphabet characters that Louis Braille had assigned, but developed many short forms or abbreviations that increased the speed with which braille could be read. American braille assigned alphabet characters to braille forms in an attempt to take into account the frequency of occurrence of English letters, with the most readily identifiable configurations assigned to the most frequently used letters. The capital sign was also developed. By 1910 books were being produced in all three codes with much duplication of effort. The American Printing

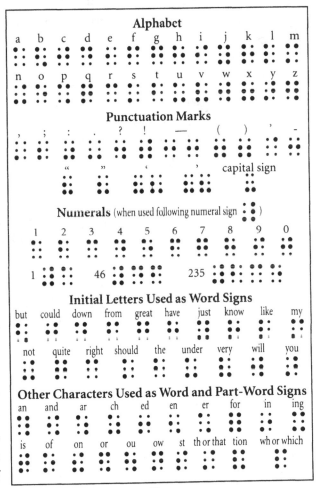

Figure 2-5. American Braille

House for the Blind (APH) initially produced books only in New York Point, but in 1910 was instructed by its board to produce 40 percent of the books in American braille as well.

THE CHOICE IS MADE

This short exposition cannot hope to capture the height of emotions and political maneuvering that were part of the war of the dots. Suffice it to say that the more recent debates over print versus braille for students with low vision have been nowhere as intense as the debates over whether New York Point, American braille, or British braille would become *the* medium for tactual reading. So how was the choice finally made?

Uniform Type Committee

In 1901, a group that soon became known as the American Association of Workers for the Blind (AAWB, now a part of the Association for Education and Rehabilitation of the Blind and Visually Impaired), passed a resolution that ultimately resulted in the formation of the Tactile Print Investigating Commission. That commission began some cursory testing of the legibility of characters, but was unsuccessful in convincing the British authorities to cooperate. The British had made substantive revisions to the code in an attempt to increase the speed of reading and writing. By 1905, revised British braille (as it was called) consisted of three grades: grade 1, fully spelled; grade 2, moderately contracted; and grade 3, highly contracted (Rodenberg, 1955). Contractions included word abbreviations and short forms.

In 1905, the AAWB formed the Uniform Type Committee to replace the Tactile Print Investigating Commission. The committee quickly rejected the use of line type, although it recognized the value of Moon type to those who had lost their vision late in life, and began a study of the three dot systems: American braille, New York Point, and British braille. It continued to do research on the three dot systems, but finally proposed a new system, standard dot, in 1914. Once standard dot was accepted in 1915 by both the AAWB and the American Association of Instructors of the Blind, the Uniform Type Committee was disbanded, and the Commission on Uniform Type for the Blind was created to carry on the work.

The standard dot system soon found disfavor, however, with its opponents referring to it as "standard rot" (Farrell, 1956, p. 112). The British dissatisfaction with this system led the American Commission on Uniform Type to adopt revised British braille in 1917, but to retain only 44 of the signs—not all the various contractions and word forms used by the British. This American revision became known as grade 1½. By now, American users of the tactual systems were tired of changes: "Many still living had first learned line type, then New York Point, then American braille, then revised braille, grade 1½" (Irwin, 1955/1970, p. 47).

Mechanization of Production

Many factors were involved in the choice of a code to be used by all people who were blind, including the legibility of the code, but the crucial factor was the development of technology to mechanize the production of the dot codes. Embossed line types could not be produced easily and were extremely bulky. The dot or point systems lent themselves much more readily to mechanization. In 1892, Frank Hall invented the Hall braillewriter, which he used to produce American braille, and then proceeded to develop the braille stereotyper, which could emboss metal plates that could be used to produce multiple copies of pages for book production. In 1894, William Wait countered by producing the Kleidograph to handle New York Point. The development of technology for writing the code to be used in reading assured the success of the dot codes over the print line type and provided for the two components of literacy—reading and writing—once and for all. Several different dot codes still existed, however, with much duplication of effort.

Standard English Braille

One of the findings of the Uniform Type Committee was that British readers of grade 2 braille were slowed down when they read American grade 1½ braille, supposedly because they were encountering characters and words in forms to which they were unaccustomed. Another finding was that students in Canada who used the British grade 2 system were superior readers to students in the United States who used either New York Point or American braille. Americans began to order books from England and saw the advantage of reading with greater speed. Through the efforts of persons who were blind, an agreement, known as the Treaty of London, was signed in 1932 by representatives of the English-speaking countries, to make revised British braille, grade 2, the medium of reading and writing for blind people. Standard English braille, grade 2 (as it is now known) has become the standard literary code for the English-speaking countries.

The Treaty of London allowed for the printing of books in grade 2 in the United States, but it was not until the 1950s that beginning readers were introduced to braille grade 2. In *The War of the Dots*, Irwin (1955/1970, p. 52) stated:

> This slow adoption of Standard English braille grade 2 has probably resulted in a generation of poor braille readers, because the method of teaching reading has forced children to familiarize themselves with three successive groups of word forms; first, the word form presented to the finger by grade 1 (full spelling) used in the lower, primary grades; second, the word form of grade 1½ used in books below junior high school; and third, the word forms of grade 2 in which books to be used by most adults are printed.

Other Codes and Special Formats

At the time of the Treaty of London, the *music braille code*, developed by Louis Braille, was also in use, and is still used today with very few changes. Two other codes were later devised to account for specialized symbols used in mathematics and science (the *Nemeth Code*) and symbols used in computer notation (*computer code*).

Other special formats that have been developed include *foreign language braille* and *textbook format*. Foreign language braille differs from the braille used in non-English-speaking countries. It is a representation of special symbols, accent marks, and letters used in foreign languages, but is essentially based on English braille. Textbook format was established to standardize the manner in which print is represented through the use of braille.

Braille configurations in one code or format do not necessarily have the same meaning in other codes. Thus, teachers who know literary braille may or may not know the various other codes and notations.

FROM LOUIS BRAILLE'S CODE TO STANDARD ENGLISH BRAILLE

Since some readers may not be familiar with the braille system, let's look briefly at Braille's original code and the form in which it is used today. The system Braille developed was based on a six-dot cell, three points high and two points wide. Each dot was assigned a numerical name. It was possible to arrange these dots into 63 configurations plus one space. "His construction of signs was systematic in the extreme, though brilliant and simple" (Rodenberg, 1955, p. 5). Braille used the 63 configurations in the following manner:

Alphabet letters (French)	25
Accent marks (French)	15
Addition of letter w	1
Punctuation marks	10
Mathematical signs	10
Special signs (composition)	2

With some adaptations, particularly the elimination of the accent signs, this is the code first used in the United States in 1860 at the Missouri School for the Blind and in Great Britain in 1868. Figure 2-6 shows the progressive construction of the 63 cells as they are identified in the *current* code. A few new signs and rule changes have been added to the code since standard English braille was adopted in 1932. In the United States and Canada, changes related to the use of several contractions and other signs were made in 1980, 1987, and 1991. Currently, braille configurations are assigned as follows:

Alphabet letters	26
Accent mark	1
Punctuation marks	20
Mathematical signs	10
Special composition signs	10
Whole-word signs	
One-cell	43
Two-cell	33
Part-word signs	
One-cell	23
Two-cell	14
Short-form words	76

Line one characters are formed of dots 1, 2, 4, & 5, in the upper part of the cell.

Line 1	⠁	⠃	⠉	⠙	⠑	⠋	⠛	⠓	⠊	⠚
Letters	a	b	c	d	e	f	g	h	i	j
Numbers	1	2	3	4	5	6	7	8	9	0

Line two adds dot 3 to each of the characters of line one.

Line 2	⠅	⠇	⠍	⠝	⠕	⠏	⠟	⠗	⠎	⠞
	k	l	m	n	o	p	q	r	s	t

Line three adds dots 3 & 6 to each of the characters of line one. Note there is no "w" in the French alphabet. "W" was added later.

Line 3	⠥	⠧	⠭	⠽	⠵	and	for	of	the	with
	u	v	x	y	z	and	for	of	the	with

Line four adds dot 6 to each of the characters of line one.

Line 4	ch	gh	sh	th	wh	ed	er	ou	ow	w
	ch	gh	sh	th	wh	ed	er	ou	ow	w

Line five repeats line one in the lower part of the cell with dots 2, 3, 5, 6.

Line 5	ea	be	con	dis	en	to	were	his	in	was
	ea	be	con	dis	en	to	were	his	in	was

Lines 6 and 7 use the remaining combinations and the space. They have many meanings serving as part-words, punctuation and prefixes.

Line 6	st	ing	ble	ar	apostrophe	com
	st	ing	ble	ar	apostrophe	com

Line 7	dot 4	dots 4-5	dots 4-5-6	dot 5	dots 4-6	dots 5-6
	dot 4	dots 4-5	dots 4-5-6	dot 5	dots 4-6	dots 5-6

Figure 2-6. The Braille Seven-Line Chart. Source: *New Programmed Instruction in Braille*, by S. C. Ashcroft, F. M. Henderson, L. R. Sanford, & A. J. Koenig, 1991, Nashville, TN: SCALARS. Copyright © 1991, SCALARS. Reprinted by permission.

Since there are only 63 possible configurations, each configuration has multiple uses; indeed, some have as many as four uses. To clarify the multiple uses of a single configuration, a complex set of rules has been established. To achieve literacy, the person who is blind must learn the uses of each configuration and the rules that govern it.

While standard English braille was being considered, committees from both the United States and the United Kingdom worked to develop an appropriate code. Currently, the Braille Authority of North America (BANA) and the Braille Authority of the United Kingdom (BAUK) fill such roles.

SUMMARY

This brief history of literacy for people who are blind or visually impaired shows how far we have travelled since the days when people who were blind were forced into institutions or compelled to beg for their very existence. It took a change in attitudes toward the capabilities of blind people for them to be considered educable; and then it required the development and subsequent acceptance of a single tactile system of reading and writing that they could use successfully for that literacy to be truly realized. Even more recently, technological advances have allowed greater access to braille materials. Today, people who are blind or visually impaired can have braille copies of print materials with the touch of a computer keystroke.

When one considers the struggle that took place to obtain this form of reading and writing, it is ironic that some people today feel braille is no longer needed—that it can be replaced by the new equipment that translates directly from print into speech. But that equipment does not allow for precisely what blind people were struggling so hard to achieve: the ability to read and write independently and privately and to communicate directly with the written material on the page—in other words, to be the sole interpreter of the information provided. Braille is literacy for people who are blind.

REFERENCES

Farrell, G. (1956). *The story of blindness.* Cambridge: Harvard University Press.

French, R. S. (1932). *From Homer to Helen Keller.* New York: American Foundation for the Blind.

Gaur, A. (1992). *A history of writing.* New York: Cross River Press.

Illingworth, W. H. (1910). *History of the education of the blind.* London: Sampson Low, Marston & Co.

Irwin, R. B. (1970). *The war of the dots.* New York: American Foundation for the Blind. (Originally published in Irwin, R. B. (1955). *As I saw it.* New York: American Foundation for the Blind.)

Newman, S. E., and Hall, A. D. (1988). Ease of learning the Braille and Fishburne alphabets. *Journal of Visual Impairment & Blindness, 82,* 148-149.

Rodenberg, L. W. (1955). *The story of embossed books for the blind.* New York: American Foundation for the Blind.

Shafrath, M. R. (1986). An alternative to braille labeling. *Journal of Visual Impairment & Blindness, 80,* 955-956.

CHAPTER 3

LEARNING PROCESSES OF PEOPLE WHO ARE BLIND

There are countless similarities in teaching children who are blind and children with normal vision to read and write, as well as countless similarities in the way that blind and sighted children learn. However, there are also unique aspects in the way children who are blind learn and hence in the way that they are taught. This chapter addresses certain aspects of tactual and visual reading and writing—including the development of language; the development of sensory discrimination and perception; the use of touch; and the role of memory, movement, and assimilation—and relates them to learning braille.

LANGUAGE

The first stage of literacy learning, now commonly referred to as emergent literacy, was once called the reading-readiness stage. The cornerstone of emergent literacy is language. Children develop language by listening to the spoken words of others and by repeating those words. If children observe the literacy activities of others, they realize the relationship between the spoken word and the written word.

By listening to and mimicking the speech of others, children eventually learn pronunciation, syntax (grammar), and semantics (meaning). These three components of language form the linguistic basis of literacy, which is discussed in Chapter 4. The child who is blind may need additional time and experiences to develop these aspects of language, especially the semantic component.

During the emergent literacy stage, children develop concepts while they are learning language; these concepts foster their ability to use the semantic elements of literacy. Both language development and concept development continue as children progress to other stages of literacy learning. They constitute important aspects of the individual schema necessary for successful reading and writing. The roles of language, concepts, and schema are discussed in Chapters 4 and 5.

Since young children who are blind do not have incidental opportunities to observe the reading and writing activities of those around them, care must be taken to alert them that such activities are taking place (see "Activities That Promote Emergent Literacy in Young Children Who Are Blind" in Chapter 1). Thus, they should be given braille books, particularly braille copies of stories that are being read to them, and encouraged to scribble with a slate and stylus and with a braillewriter, as children with normal vision scribble with pencils and crayons. In addition, parents and teachers can let children know when they are making lists, writing letters and notes to friends and other family members, or engaging in other literacy activities.

SENSORY DISCRIMINATION AND PERCEPTION

Without doubt, the most unique aspect of literacy learning by children who are blind is their use of touch for reading what they or others have written. For reading, the sensory organ is usually a finger or fingers of one or both hands. The tactual sensory organs are part of a complex and elaborate system linked to the brain; a sophisticated intermediate system of analyzers and filters refines the signal before it arrives in the brain. The tactual sense is a dynamic one with its own characteristics. Unfortunately, some unique characteristics of touch, such as the ability to discriminate volume, temperature, size, and texture, are only slightly involved in learning to read. However, information related to these characteristics is useful as the child develops related language and concepts; such development provides the knowledge and schema necessary for competence in reading braille.

Unlike the visual sense, which allows for simultaneous perceptions of various aspects of a single object or concept, the tactual sense requires that information must be derived by the exploration of one aspect at a time. The learner must engage in multiple explorations to gain information comparable to that gained by the sighted learner in a single viewing. If either the quality or quantity of these explorations is inadequate, the knowledge and experience necessary for the learner's successful interaction with the reading text may not be adequate for reading a particular passage.

Learners who are blind have to be taught to use touch, just as sighted learners are taught to use vision. However, opportunities for incidental learning through the sense of touch are limited and hence must be consciously provided and encouraged. Children who are blind are not distracted by objects around them and therefore do not learn about those objects unless they are given the opportunity and are encouraged to explore their surroundings. Without such encouragement and opportunities, blind children often become passive receivers of whatever happens to come their way instead of engaging in the active exploration and experimentation that is necessary for the full development of their sense of touch (Hampshire, 1975).

**SEQUENCE OF TACTUAL
DISCRIMINATION TASKS
FOR LEARNERS WHO ARE BLIND**

1. Large, solid geometric figures.

2. Flat figures, smaller than in Task 1.

3. Embossed-dot geometric figures, smaller than in Tasks 1 or 2.

4. Embossed-dot line figures.

5. Braille figures.

Source: Based on "A Hierarchy of Tasks in the Development of Tactual Discrimination" by S. M. Kershman, 1976, *Education of the Visually Handicapped, 13,* pp. 98-108.

Teachers can help children become active explorers of their surroundings, such as the objects displayed during "show and tell" and the unfamiliar surroundings on a field trip. Teachers should assist children to go beyond mere awareness of their environment to use their sense of touch efficiently and effectively.

Despite the importance of the sense of touch in literacy learning by children who are blind, there has been little theory or research in this area. However, one useful finding related to literacy learning is Kershman's (1976) identification of a hierarchy of tactual discrimination tasks. This hierarchy includes a sequence of five tasks that progress from the level of beginning awareness and attention to the level of braille symbology. The teacher who follows this sequence during the emergent literacy stage can prepare a child to function as an active explorer and learner. When the child moves to the use of braille symbols, touch can be further refined for concept development and comprehension, as well as for increased speed of reading and writing.

MEMORY SYSTEM
IN TACTUAL INFORMATION PROCESSING

Every teacher knows the importance of memory in learning, including literacy learning. Nursery rhymes and poems, children's storybooks, and even the basal readers that many teachers still use repeat words and phrases. Children memorize the language of these materials and repeat them in their first efforts to read and write. Essentially, the memory system of children who learn tactually does not differ from the memory system of those who learn visually. However, the tactual memory system has unique aspects that influence the way children who are blind learn. This system is divided into three stages: (1) the sensory register, (2) short-term memory store, and (3) long-term memory store.

Sensory Register

Information from tactual explorations is received by the sensory register, which has a large, almost infinite, capacity. The capacity of the *tactual sensory register* is somewhat smaller than that of the *visual sensory register*. Information in the visual sensory register decays in one or two seconds, whereas information in the tactual register decays in just over a second. Information from the sensory register is coded into the short-term memory store, the working memory.

Short-Term Memory Store

Since decay takes place in the sensory register, not all the information it receives is coded into the short-term memory store. In addition, the capacity of the short-term memory store is sharply limited, considerably smaller than that of the sensory register. The span of the visual short-term memory store is four digits at age 4 and five to six digits at age 11 and increases to six or seven discrete digits for the typical adult (hence the seven-digit telephone number and the five-digit zip code). As the working memory, the short-term memory manipulates and compares material, which it either discards or recodes into meaning at a highly abstracted level (Thorndike, 1984). Thorndike (pp. 17-19) identified several important facts regarding the working memory:

1. Memory span is a function that increases with age.
2. Memory span is a function of the type of material.
3. Grouping—or "chunking"—is important in determining the amount of material of a given type that working memory can cope with.
4. The size of the memory span is related to general ability (cognitive) measures.

Long-Term Memory Store

The material coded and reorganized in the short-term memory store is then placed in the long-term memory store. The contents of long-term memory constitute one of the important determiners of the ability to carry out cognitive tasks, including literacy learning.

Most information and research about the role of memory in literacy learning is related to visual memory. The work that has been done in the area of tactual memory has concluded that information is processed in essentially the same way in the visual and tactual modes (Bliss & Crane, 1969; Hill & Bliss, 1968). The smaller capacity of the working tactual memory and the somewhat more rapid rate of decay of information certainly have implications for instruction in literacy. Memory plays an important role in the development of language, concepts, and reading and writing skills. Thus, teachers must provide children who are blind with sufficient and appropriate opportunities, from the concrete to the symbolic, to fill their memory stores and to utilize what has been stored.

"CHUNKING" PROCESS

A process of assimilation or "chunking" occurs during reading. Chunking is the grouping of elements to form a unit—letters are chunked to form words and words to form phrases or sentences. Young sighted readers can chunk 7 to 10 letters, and the number increases with age and practice. Beginning print readers chunk letters to form words in a single fixation, starting with 2-to-3-letter words and progressing to 7-to-10-letter words in the first year of instruction. By the time they have reached such competence with letters, they are also chunking two or three short words (Thorndike, 1984). The ability to chunk words and phrases has a direct effect on the learner's rate of reading, as well as on comprehension.

It is known that readers who are blind have the ability to group letters perceptually into words, phrases, and sentences (Bliss & Crane, 1969). Good braille readers can chunk braille characters, whereas poor readers read one braille character at a time (Kusajima, 1974). Although the ability exists to group symbols of whatever nature, it must be recognized that this task goes beyond the perceptual level to include the higher level of cognitive functioning for the reader who is blind as well as the reader with normal vision (Hampshire, 1975; Thorndike, 1984).

PERCEPTUAL UNIT IN BRAILLE READING

The lack of simultaneous perceptions that was mentioned as a limitation of tactual perception has major implications in the reading process of learners who are blind. The extensive investigation by APH into the perceptual factors in braille word recognition found that "the unit in braille word recognition seems to be the braille character" (Nolan & Kederis, 1969, p. 38). In other words, the perceptual unit was found to be a single cell.

When the ability of sighted readers to chunk (perceive) 2 to 10 letters in a single fixation is compared to the ability of blind readers to perceive a single cell of braille, one can understand why children who are blind may read more slowly than do children with normal vision. However, those who have done comprehensive investigations of the braille reading process (Kolers, 1972; Kusajima, 1974) have emphasized that reading is not merely perception, but perception combined with the ability to use such peripheral cues as context, expectation, and stored information during reading.

Instruction in braille reading and writing may also account for the differences in comprehension and rate. The limited perceptual unit of braille tends to direct the reader—and often disposes the teacher to instruct the child—to read cell by cell. Rather, the reader should be encouraged to "think" in chunks and to utilize the redundant parts of words and sentences, which will increase the rate of reading and improve comprehension. Good language development, good concept development, and good tactual development provide the reader with a well-developed schema and the ability to utilize his or her cognitive skills.

MOVEMENT

Movement is another unique aspect of literacy learning for people who are blind. Whereas visual reading takes place when the eye is at rest and the perceptual span of an eye fixation relates directly to the number of symbols perceived during chunking, tactual reading takes place only if movement occurs. Smooth and rhythmic hand movements that utilize redundancy and the ability to concentrate on key portions of words and phrases can offset the limitation of the single cell as the tactual perceptual unit. Hand movement patterns are discussed in Chapter 6.

VISUAL COMPARED TO TACTUAL READING

During the 1960s and 1970s, when braille was the major literacy medium for most persons who were legally blind, several major studies compared visual and tactual reading (Hampshire, 1975; Kusajima, 1974; Nolan & Kederis, 1969). These studies concluded that there are vast similarities in visual and tactual reading. These similarities provide justification for including learners who use braille in classrooms with those who read print. The similarities in learning should ensure that regular classroom teachers can assume a role in the literacy instruction of their students who are blind. However, since there are indeed some differences, the regular teacher and the blind learner need the assistance of a competent special educator who can adapt literacy instruction to take the unique aspects into account. The special educator must be trained to teach literacy, be competent in reading and writing the braille code, and be able to incorporate instruction related to the braille code into the instruction for reading and writing by the student who is blind.

THE BRAILLE CODE

Earlier, it was stated that use of the tactual sense was the most unique aspect of literacy learning for people who are blind. Implicit in this notion is the use of the braille code as the mode of reading and writing. Braille is a system in which characters are portrayed graphically by embossed dots that are presented in units called cells. Each cell contains one to six dots. A full cell has two vertical columns of three dots:

$$\begin{matrix} \bullet & \bullet \\ \bullet & \bullet \\ \bullet & \bullet \end{matrix}$$

As noted earlier, all letters, digits, and symbols of print must be portrayed in braille using only the 63 possible configurations of dots. These configurations may be extended in a number of ways:
- by combining two or more cells to function as a single unit.
- by the multiple use of any cell (for example, the configuration for the letter *d* also functions as the digit *4* and as the word *do*).
- by special composition signs.

It is possible to make a literal translation of print to braille by using the various configurations. However, to do so, one must follow special rules that determine the use of the various signs to portray characters in literary, mathematical and scientific, or musical presentations.

Braille Is Not a Language

With the many unique aspects of the conventional braille system, some have argued, albeit with no foundation, that braille is a language. Braille is *not* a language; since it is a portrayal of print, with special rules and multiple uses of each sign (configuration), it is a code. English is the language, one that can be conveyed in any number of ways as long as the code is systematic and is agreed to by those who use it. Both the conventional graphic system (print) and conventional tactual system (braille) meet these basic requirements. (One has only to consider the disarray caused by the "war of the dots" to understand the requirement and necessity for common agreement on the use of any code.) Print and braille are equally effective systems for conveying a writer's message to an audience through the language of English. Other conventional systems, such as Morse code and Moon type, are also effective communication systems, but still convey messages through the English language. As mentioned, there are different codes for the braille user—literary, mathematical or scientific, and musical—as well as a computer code. This chapter is concerned with the braille literary code—the code used for reading and writing.

Intricacy of the Braille Code

Braille is both intricate and complex, but it has allowed many people who are blind, both children and adults, to become literate. It is the way in which individuals who are blind communicate best with themselves and receive communication from others that may not be provided as efficiently in an aural manner.

Hampshire (1975, p. 151) identified the most obvious cognitive variable in learning to read braille as "the often difficult task of decoding braille symbols." The braille code may mask, confuse, or contradict the cues that normally allow the beginning reader to encode the language patterns that facilitate efficient reading, as shown in the accompanying examples of inconsistencies of the braille code.

Hampshire noted "that the braille code itself is responsible to a large extent for the slowness of braille reading, and not [the fact] that braille is read tactually rather than visually" (p. 151). The compatibility of the braille symbols and the units into which language is

---

EXAMPLES OF INCONSISTENCIES OF THE BRAILLE CODE

- **Masking**

    Distortion of the base word:
    do in *do*ing, un*do*
    total in tot*ally*
    child in *child*re*n* (chn)

    Use of double letters in base word plus prefix or suffix:
    egg, egg*s*
    puff, pu*ff*ing

- **Confusing**

    Dual spelling of words:
    Full spelling or contracted
    in, were, his

    Choice of contraction:
    ever or *every* in
    *every*day, *every* day, *every*-day

- **Contradicting**

    Use of braille signs in relation to pronunciation

    Use of braille signs in relation to syllabication

coded when it is read or written must be optimized. Hampshire suggested further study to determine which units of the language code, particularly its syntactical or grammatical units, are not compatible with the braille code. Unfortunately, such research has not been conducted, perhaps because of decreased focus on braille reading at both the instructional and the reader levels.

An analysis, based on linguistic principles, conducted by Hamp and Caton (1984) presented a set of the elements of braille and examined the terms used to describe them. Hamp and Caton described some familiar terms in a more meaningful way, and added some new ones. They replaced some familiar terms, such as "contraction," with more descriptive terms, such as "shape" or "braille unit." Such terms are intended to help teachers "describe and discuss any element of the braille code in a manner easily understood by children" (p. 214). Unfortunately, teachers and others, including the authors of this book, have not completely made the transition to the new terms. It is not a matter of opposition to the terms but, rather, the tendency to be comfortable with the old ones. Hamp and Caton also caution that the teaching of braille reading and print reading are not truly analogous. An understanding of the internal characteristics of the braille code would "provide teachers with more effective strategies for teaching reading to children who use braille as their primary media" (p. 214).

Both teachers and children encounter the inconsistencies found in reading braille. Good teachers use strategies to provide the knowledge and experience needed to overcome the incompatibility between the language code and the braille code. Such strategies involve being alert to the inconsistencies and presenting additional materials—reading texts and learning activities—that focus on the rules related to the inconsistencies. If sufficient opportunities are provided, the information will be placed in the long-term memory store, and both comprehension and speed of braille reading will increase. Other strategies and materials can focus on the redundancy of the language and using the context of the story to help comprehend it. Later chapters and *Instructional Strategies for Braille Literacy* (Swallow & Wormsley, in press), a companion volume, will provide ideas and suggestions for additional materials. Teachers must not let the intricacies of the code prevent them from providing literacy learning to those who are capable of learning to read and to write in the braille medium.

SUMMARY

The way children who are blind learn—both general learning and literacy learning—is more similar to the learning of children with normal vision than it is different, in terms of the development of language and concepts, sensory discrimination and perception, and the memory system. There are differences, however, particularly in regard to the need to provide opportunities to observe reading and writing, the use of touch as the chief sensory organ for reading, and the limitations in size of the perceptual unit and the ability to group (chunk) symbols in braille. Understanding these similarities and differences is a crucial first step to formulating strategies to teach literacy through braille reading and writing.

REFERENCES

Bliss, J. C., & Crane, H. D. (1969). Tactile perception. *American Foundation for the Blind Research Bulletin, 19,* 269-274.

Hamp, E. P., & Caton, H. (1984). A fresh look at the sign system of the braille code. *Journal of Visual Impairment & Blindness, 78,* 210-214.

Hampshire, B. (1975). Tactile and visual reading. *The New Outlook for the Blind, 69,* 145-154.

Hill, J. W., & Bliss, J. (1968). Modeling a tactile sensory register. *American Foundation for the Blind Research Bulletin, 17,* 91-136.

Kershman, S. M. (1976). A hierarchy of tasks in the development of tactual discrimination: Part one. *Education of the Visually Handicapped, 13,* 98-108.

Kolers, P. A. (1972). Sensory supplementation: Reading. In M. Graham (Ed.), *Science and blindness: Retrospective and prospective.* New York: American Foundation for the Blind.

Kusajima, T. (1974). *Visual reading and braille reading: An experimental investigation of the physiology and psychology of visual and tactual reading.* (L. L. Clark & Z. S. Jastrembska, Trans.). New York: American Foundation for the Blind.

Nolan, C. Y., & Kederis, C. J. (1969). *Perceptual factors in braille word recognition. Research series, No. 20.* New York: American Foundation for the Blind.

Swallow, R.M., & Wormsley, D.P. (in press). *Instructional strategies for braille literacy.* New York: AFB Press.

Thorndike, R. L. (1984). *Intelligence as information processing: The mind and the computer.* Bloomington, IN: Phi Delta Kappa.

CHANGING VIEWS ON TEACHING READING AND WRITING

During the past decade, theoretical and classroom-related research on the reading and writing processes and effective reading and writing strategies has led to a change in the philosophy of and approaches to literacy instruction (see Anderson, Hiebert, Scott, & Wilkinson, 1985, for a summary). These changes—from the skills-centered approach to the meaning-centered approach—have led to a renewed interest in such questions as What are reading and writing? What are the major components of the reading and writing processes? How do children learn to read and to write? What are effective teaching-learning strategies for literacy instruction? and What are the special considerations for reading and writing instruction when the learner is blind and uses braille as the mode for literacy? This chapter presents background information on reading and writing in general and the various viewpoints on reading and writing processes. Interwoven with this information are implications of the current status of reading and writing for students who are blind.

Earlier chapters reflected the philosophy of the authors in focusing on literacy as a single and unified concept. However, there are enough differences in the processes of teaching reading and writing—the two components of literacy—to justify treating them separately here and in the following two chapters on instructional approaches and strategies.

READING

Changing Roles of Teachers

Just as regular teachers are undergoing a transition in their philosophies toward teaching and in their teaching practices, so are teachers of children who are blind. With more and more blind students being included in the regular classroom, the roles of these teachers are changing significantly. Some teachers are beginning to function less as reading teachers of children who are blind and more as consultants and members of reading teams. Since many itinerant teachers work in several schools, and often in several school districts, they may work with regular classroom teachers at all stages of transition. As members of these cooperative reading teams, they become both learners and teachers. Although these new team roles will be challenging at times, if not frustrating, they will ultimately be rewarding when the students who are blind become literate in reading and writing in braille.

To illustrate how the instruction of children who are blind is integrated into the teaching of reading and writing in the regular classroom, consider the accompanying true scenario of

---

TIM IS LEARNING TO READ AND WRITE

THE LEARNER

Tim is a totally blind 6 year old. He is an active, alert, inquisitive boy of average intelligence and adequate language development for a first grader. He is a personable child and likes school, his teachers, and learning to read.

THE TEACHERS

Tim is in a special education program for children who are blind. His first-grade teacher, Ms. Andrews, has been prepared well to teach first grade and especially enjoys teaching reading to her group of approximately 25 children. Her enjoyment and competence are evident as we observe her.

Tim is the only blind child in the group, and he has a second teacher, Ms. Blakely, an itinerant teacher, who comes to Lincoln School for two hours a day to provide assistance to Tim, Ms. Andrews, and the other children in Tim's class. Ms. Blakely is also competent and well prepared for her role. She became a certified teacher of students with visual impairment about 15 years ago, but then left teaching for several years to start her family. This is her second year back, and she is now an itinerant teacher rather than the resource room teacher she once was. When Ms. Blakely returned to teaching, she also began work on a master's degree with an emphasis on reading instruction. We can see that she enjoys working with children and especially enjoys teaching Tim and the others to read.

THE SETTING

Tim attends first grade in a typical school. He spends most of the day in the regular class. He and Ms. Blakely retreat to their little cubbyhole for 20 to 30 minutes each day.

Most of this scenario takes place in the regular classroom, which looks like any typical first-grade classroom, just as Tim and the other children look and act like a typical group of first graders. The uniqueness of this setting is the presence of two

(continued on next page)

Tim, a braille reader, who receives reading instruction from both a regular and a special educator. Tim is not a gifted child, but average or slightly above average. As the scenario demonstrates, Tim, although blind, is much like his classmates with normal vision. However, Tim uses the braille medium, not print, to read and uses his fingers, rather than his eyes, while reading. This use of the tactual modality and the braille medium implies some differences in how he learns to read. The scenario also shows that instructional practices that are effective in teaching children with normal vision to read and write are also effective with blind learners. The reader should note that the key word in this scenario is *teachers*. Tim's attitude and mastery are the result of their efforts.

---

teachers and a student teacher and the way in which they function as a team, trading roles and responsibilities effortlessly and smoothly.

THE STRATEGY
The children have had a shared experience. They talked about it extensively and decided to write a shared story about it. The children "wrote" the story by dictating it to one of the teachers. They did their first writing in three small groups, and the dictated story was a composite edition of the groups' efforts. One of the teachers printed the story on the ever-present chart paper. As that teacher worked in print, Ms. Blakely sat next to Tim and wrote the story in braille. When the story was complete, the children read it through and were encouraged to revise and edit their story. All this took several sessions.

With the focus on writing completed, the edited story was both printed and brailled. Then the children and Ms. Andrews first read the story as a large group, with Tim reading from his braille copy with Ms. Blakely sitting beside him.

The children's next learning task is to find a key word in each sentence. Since this is a new technique for them, they worked a sentence at a time. As the discussion determines a key word, one child goes to the easel and put a circle around that word. Tim has his turn, finding it first on his braille copy, then walking proudly to the easel and circling the word with Ms. Andrews's guidance. He is beaming when he returns to his table.

The teachers have prepared individual copies of the story. The children are then free to read the story individually or in twos or threes. The teachers circulate about the room to provide help when the children ask for it.

Following this session, Ms. Blakely and Tim move to their private space. Tim takes a little break to work off some of his stored-up energy. Then he is ready for more reading. During these sessions, Ms. Blakely uses the *Patterns* materials for some of the "participatory" activities. She uses some of its stories and the library books for Tim's individualized reading, but Tim is not moving story by story through the series. Of course, this time is also used to help Tim infer and think about some of the rules of the braille code. He has just written his own two-line poem and brailled it with Ms. Blakely's help. He also sings it.

Viewpoints on the Reading Process

Chapter 1 introduced the concept of literacy learning and emphasized two points of view related to reading:

- Reading is part of an *integrated language process* and is not a discrete skill isolated from writing, listening, and speaking.
- Literacy learning, or language development, is a *lifelong developmental process* that begins at birth and continues to develop throughout life.

This chapter introduces several additional points of view regarding the reading process:

- Reading is a *constructive, interactive process* that focuses on constructing meaning from text.
- Reading is a *psycholinguistic process* in which readers make use of graphophonemic, syntactic, and semantic cues in their attempts to predict or construct meaning.
- Reading is a *strategic process* in which readers adapt their reading strategies according to their knowledge, purpose in reading, and the difficulty of the material.

Reading: A Constructive, Interactive Process

The current view of reading stresses that reading is a *constructive, interactive* process in which the reader interacts with the text within a certain learning context, based on his or her schema (knowledge, background, and experience) (Baker & Shaw-Baker, 1992) (see Figure 4-1). If the reader has adequate knowledge, background, and experience about the topic to be read, he or she is better able to construct meaning. Conversely, if the reader lacks knowledge, background, and experience about the topic to be read, he or she will be restricted to reproducing the literal, factual textual information over a short time.

To illustrate this concept, read the accompanying passage on "How to Build a New Model Thurboflyer" once orally and once silently and then attempt to answer the questions that follow the passage without looking back.

Now that you have read the passage and attempted to answer the questions, ask yourself the basic question: "Did I read the passage?" If you are similar to the several hundred others who have been exposed to this passage, your responses will vary. Some of you may have responded yes because you were able to *decode* (produce the oral equivalent of the printed

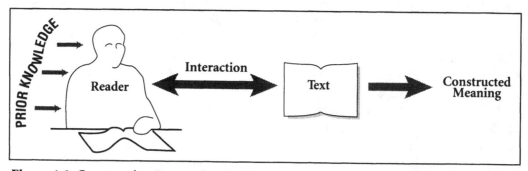

Figure 4-1. Constructive, Interactive Reading. Source: "Implementing Holistic Literacy Strategies in Chinese Teacher Preparation Programs," by R. Baker and M. Shaw-Baker, paper presented at the International Reading Association 14th World Congress on Reading, Maui, HI, July 1992.

HOW TO BUILD A NEW MODEL THURBOFLYER

First, check your materials. Make sure that your graffles are safely in a glass container and that the folutes all line up in proper sequence: first the lesnics, then the raptiforms, and last the cresnites. Keep the hygrolated maribirne hanging on the wall where it belongs.

Then check your tools. Adjust the scorp for fine work by firmly letching the small blet found behind the alapat. Sharpen the wimble and rub a little paronated bengoe into it. Screep the loors; harpen the longer of your two chamlets, leaving the other in normal position for slaping; and finally brust your strongest and toughest lollicapop. This is too often overlooked or taken for granted.

When ready to begin construction, lay out your folutes in the usual fashion, checking with your sabble-hubble until they sadiculate perfectly with each other. Then loofen them firmly, one at a time.

Directions: Answer each of the following questions as briefly as possible. Do not look back at the passage.

1. What materials must be placed in a glass container? _____

2. Name the three major types of folutes needed for constructing thurboflyers.

   _____

3. Which maribirne must be left on the wall? _____

4. How are scorps typically adjusted to allow for fine, detailed work? _____

   _____

5. Where is the small blet located? _____

6. What type of bengoe is applied during the preparation of the wimble?

   _____

7. Why must loors always be screeped? _____

8. Which chamlet must be left unharpened? _____

9. Name the tool that allows you to check the sadiculation of your folutes.

   _____

10. On the basis of your reading, briefly describe one modification in thurboflyer construction that may improve the cost-efficiency of production.

    _____

    _____

    _____

—Author unknown

word) nearly all the words in the nonsense passage. Indeed, most mature readers have mastered the basic letter-sound (*graphophonic*) relationships of the English language. As a result, you were able to pronounce terms, such as *thurboflyer, graffles, lesnics,* and *raptiforms.*

Furthermore, because of your knowledge of the grammatical structures and sentence patterns (*syntax*) of the English language, you knew that graffles, lesnics, and raptiforms are nouns; that hygrolated and paronated are adjectives; and that letching, screep, and brust are verbs. Your knowledge of grammar allowed you to predict the syntax of unknown words within the context of familiar words, even though you did not know what the words meant.

Despite the fact that you pronounced the passage correctly and were able to predict the grammatical structures within each sentence unit, you probably responded no to the question, "Did I read the passage?" More than 9 out of 10 readers have answered no because they could not understand the semantic relationships within the passage, even when given extra time to reread and study it. As Smith (1976, 1978) has indicated, reading without meaning or comprehension is nonsense.

Why were you unable to comprehend the passage? Have you ever seen a thurboflyer? Can you picture what a thurboflyer looks like? Have you ever read anything about thurboflyers? Have any of your family members or friends discussed thurboflyers with you? Do you know what lesnics, raptiforms, and cresnites are? Have you ever screeped, harpened, or brusted anything? At this time, are you interested in thurboflyers? Do you feel motivated to continue reading about them?

Simply stated, you lacked the knowledge and background experience (schema) needed to interact with the text passage to construct your own meaning or interpretation. At best, you may have been able to memorize enough information to respond to a few of the questions and thus to have reproduced the text's exact meaning. However, if you had been allowed to reread the passage to find answers to each of the 10 questions, you would have answered at least the first 9 questions successfully because the answers are literally, or explicitly, stated in the passage. Only Question 10 requires any thinking or application beyond the literal level. Once again, you would have simply reproduced the text's meaning without truly comprehending the passage.

To summarize, constructing meaning depends on the reader's ability to combine what he or she already knows (schema) with information presented in text materials to produce meaning unique to the reader. This constructive, interactive view of the reading process is referred to as *schema theory.*

Implications of Schema Theory in Reading Braille

The constructive, interactive reading model illustrates the importance of the learner's schema. The reader who is blind and uses braille has and needs an individual schema. Blindness may provide a dimension of uniqueness that makes an interpretation somewhat different from the individualized and unique meanings of sighted peers. However, the schema of blind readers must not be too different. Blind readers need sufficient knowledge, background, and experience to interact with the text and arrive at a meaning that is closely related to the author's intent and closely related to the meaning gained by their sighted peers.

Teachers of children who are blind have long been aware of the importance of the learner's schema, though they did not use the term. Teachers who provided instruction at the emergent or "readiness" level and at the beginning reading level were particularly aware of the need for a rich background of experiences. They were concerned about the children's concept development (knowledge) and the language and other experiences by which the children developed those concepts. As blind children progress in their reading development, the special teacher also feels a strong commitment to enhance their knowledge, including knowledge of the braille code, and to provide the needed experience for them to acquire the schema necessary to interact with each text in such a way that meaning is constructed. Most teachers trained to work with blind students are somewhat ahead of the game in their competence to help children develop their individual schemas (Rex, 1989).

Experiences

The importance of experiences to blind children was first addressed by Lowenfeld (1948/1981), who identified three objective effects of blindness. The first effect is the limitation in the range and variety of experiences. Lowenfeld wrote prolifically on this cognitive limitation, often relating the limitations to reading by blind children and to the reading instruction of those children (Lowenfeld, 1973, 1980, 1948/1981).

Experience is the core of communication. Some commonality of experience must exist between communicators. Experience is the bond in the interactive process of expressive and receptive communication. As Henderson (1973, p. 186) stated, "the school, in its program for the visually impaired student, must constantly be involved in the enrichment and expansion of experience—the core which gives birth to the desire and the skills for communication. The program should capitalize upon the strengths of tactual, kinesthetic, aural, and olfactory perception." Henderson also encouraged the use of even a small degree of vision. Earlier (1960), she cautioned against equating the experiences of children who are blind with those of sighted children. Experiences should be similar in the purposes that are achieved, rather than in the materials that are used. The actual experiences of the home and the classroom environments offer many opportunities to develop language and concepts.

From the limitations he identified, Lowenfeld (1980) derived five basic principles of teaching blind children: individualization, concreteness, unified instruction, additional stimulation, and self-activity. These principles are addressed here in light of their implications for the development of literacy by blind children in today's schools.

The principle of *individualization* is certainly put into effect as the student selects reading material based on his or her interest and is guided by the teacher as to its difficulty in terms of the braille code, other readability factors, and the student's individual schema. As the student reads silently, the teacher is present to assist when necessary. Following the reading of the story, the student and teacher hold a story conference. An added dimension of this conference may be the discussion of new braille signs and inferences to determine rules for the use of any of the signs. The integration of individual writing (a personal journal or short story) further enhances literacy as the teacher applies this first principle of instruction.

The principle of *concreteness* requires little discussion. Its importance in developing language concepts cannot be minimized for any learner. Piaget recognized the necessity of concreteness in the early stages of cognitive development (as discussed in Stephens & Grube, 1982), but its importance and use need to be extended beyond this stage for blind learners.

For literacy instruction, the principle of *unified instruction* certainly means integration of the four language-communication areas: speaking, listening, writing, and reading. It also ensures that communication skills learned in the classroom are meaningfully applied in authentic contexts elsewhere throughout the student's life. It is a principle that the authors strongly recommend.

With the principle of *additional stimulation*, "more is better"—more language, more experiences, more braille in the daily environment, more books to listen to or read, more stories to write, and more experiences to be ready to read. As additional stimulation is provided, the learner develops the schema needed at all levels.

The principle of *self-activity* may be viewed as a combination of the first four principles in literacy programs today. It certainly is applicable to the strategic reading process in which the reader monitors his or her comprehension before adapting his or her reading strategies to the task at hand.

Little has been written about the relationship of experiences to reading since Lowenfeld and Henderson wrote about its importance 20 years ago. The new emphasis on literacy focuses greater attention on young children and the foundations of literacy, the stage of emergent literacy. Experiences are certainly an important component of emergent literacy, but the importance of experiences does not decrease as literacy develops. The reader's schema, which includes experiences, continues to be an indispensable factor in reading.

Language

Meaningful language is the foundation of literacy. Oral language becomes written language. The greater the compatibility of spoken and written language, the greater the ease of reading and writing tasks.

The greatest degree of language development takes place during the stage of emergent literacy, from age 1½ to age 5 (Mills, 1983a). The need for early intervention in language development and for good role models is obvious. Intervention may be needed as much by parents, older children, and others in the blind child's environment as by the blind child.

Stratton and Wright (1991, p. 57) identified four components of emergent literacy that gradually develop into the reading-writing connection:

1. Broad experiences to build understanding for stories.
2. Language skills, including the meaning of words.
3. Listening to stories read aloud.
4. Scribbling.

Certainly the language of the reader contributes to the schema of the reading task. Component 1 has already been discussed from this perspective. Component 2 goes beyond learning words with meaning. It not only avoids words that are semantically empty, but extends the meaning of words through the interaction of language and experiences and builds concepts through this same interaction. Component 3 is considered "the single most important activity for building the knowledge required for eventual success in reading" (Anderson et al., 1985, p. 23). Component 4 encourages the manipulation of braille writing equipment to expose the child to tactual scribbling, a part of his or her developing schema and a factor in the integrated language process described in Chapter 1.

The literature related to language and the emergent literacy of blind children is rich in comparison to other areas. It has been written by parents (Miller, 1985), teachers (Blos, 1974; Swenson, 1988), teacher educators (Erin, 1986; Ferrell, 1985; Rogow, 1988), and researchers (Mills, 1983b).

The integrated language-communication model (see Figure 1-1, Chapter 1) conveys the importance of language in the communication process, particularly the interaction of the various components. It also stresses that language continues to develop throughout life. Literacy is a continuous process because an individual's schema changes daily, which permits him or her to bring new knowledge, background, and experiences to the reading task.

Concept Formation

Just as language is a necessary component of both knowledge and experience as a schema is developed, so is concept formation. Concept formation ranges from the concrete idea of an apple to its classification as a fruit to solving the problem of how to get the apple from the top of the tree. Certain concepts must be present if meaningful reading is to take place. Likewise, meaningful reading can assist in concept formation.

The relationship between language development and concept development should not be minimized, because each influences the development of the other. Both are enhanced by knowledge and experiences. Several of the investigations reported in Mills (1983b) studied the relationship of the conceptual domain (the representation by which the world is understood) and the semantic domain (knowledge of the relationships among words and word meanings). The conceptual and semantic domains are separate. Blind individuals can acquire semantic knowledge before, or without, conceptual knowledge. For example, studies have found that a blind person's use of color words represents meanings and categories that the person actually manipulates and thinks about (Cromer, 1983).

Barraga (1986) noted the importance of several factors involved in the formation of concepts and cognitive styles by children who are visually impaired:

1. Providing a range and variety of concrete experiences in the early preschool years.
2. Presenting classification and reasoning tasks throughout the school years.
3. Presenting problem-solving situations during the early years and adolescence.

Barraga suggested that "marked attention should be given to language interaction with meaningful vocabulary in discussion of thoughts and ideas to enhance the organization of thinking patterns in visually handicapped children" (p. 27). The fulfillment of this suggestion should assume that the blind learner develops an adequate schema for constructive reading.

Reading: A Psycholinguistic Process

Your experiences reading the Thurboflyer passage could be summarized from a psycholinguistic point of view (see Figure 4-2). According to Goodman (1976a, 1976b), the process of reading involves an ongoing interaction between thinking (psycho) processes and language (linguistic) processes in which the reader constantly strives to attain meaning. Goodman (1976b) referred to the act of reading as a "psycholinguistic guessing game," in which the reader makes use of available psycholinguistic cues to obtain meaning.

Within the context of the Thurboflyer passage, it seems accurate to say that you, as a reader, actively used graphophonemic cues to predict the pronunciation of words. Your awareness of grammatical relationships also provided cues for predicting the ordering of words, parts of speech, and sentence patterns. However, you were unable to predict meaning or attach meaning to the passage because nothing in your knowledge, background, or experiences was related to the nonsense words in the passage.

Implications of the Psycholinguistic Process for Learners Who Are Blind

The psycholinguistic process of reading is applicable to reading both braille and print. It has not had as much application in braille reading, perhaps because the single braille cell as the unit of perception no doubt prompts teachers to emphasize the graphophonemic aspect of the psycholinguistic process.

The psycholinguistic process relies on the redundancy of any language, such as the redundant *u* that usually follows *q*. The faster reader ignores the *u*. Redundancy does not exist in the braille code, though there is some redundancy in the graphophonemic use of the code as it is used for braille reading. Both syntactical redundancy and semantic redundancy provide cues in reading braille, since the grammar of our language is filled with redundancy, whether it is spoken, written, heard, or read in any of the symbol systems used. Aside from the redundancy, syntax provides other cues for meaningful reading. The reader can "guess" that the word that follows is a noun and from the context may also "guess" the word. The semantics of our language also provide cues through

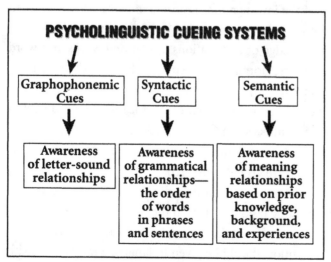

Figure 4-2. Psycholinguistic Cueing Systems

semantic redundancy and through knowledge, background, and experiences that bring meaning to the context.

Reading: A Strategic Process

Reading is also a strategic process in which good readers adapt their reading strategies according to their knowledge, their purpose in reading, and the difficulty of the materials being read (Baker & Shaw-Baker, 1992) (see Figure 4-3). Good readers constantly monitor their comprehension of text according to these three factors. This ability to monitor their own comprehension and adapt reading strategies to the task at hand is referred to as *metacognition.*

Using Figure 4-3 as a reference, ask yourself how you would read each of the following reading materials, keeping in mind your knowledge and purpose in reading and the anticipated difficulty of the reading materials:

- a recipe for baking an apple pie
- a textbook chapter on inferential statistics
- the front page of your daily newspaper
- a *Time* magazine analysis of the presidential election
- a psychology textbook the night before a final examination
- an IRS 1040 tax-preparation form
- a romance novel
- a map of major buildings and streets
- *Huckleberry Finn*
- "How to Repair Malfunctioning Thurboflyers"
- a professional journal article on the history of braille
- this chapter.

Predictably, your strategies for reading each type of material would differ considerably, depending on your knowledge and experiences of the various topics. In addition, your interests would vary on the basis of your experiences or lack of experiences. Your purposes in reading would also vary widely, from reading to fulfill certain academic requirements, to

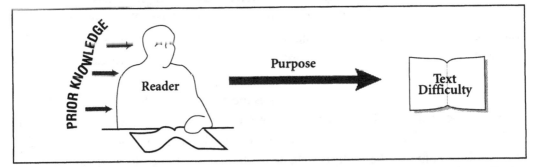

Figure 4-3. Strategic Reading. Source: "Implementing Holistic Literacy Strategies in Chinese Teacher Preparation Programs," by R. Baker and M. Shaw-Baker, paper presented at the International Reading Association 14th World Congress on Reading, Maui, HI, July 1992.

reading to gain general information, to reading to complete specific tasks, to reading for pure enjoyment. Some readings would be required; others would be self-selected. Some readings would involve pressured learning situations; others would be totally relaxing. Some readings would involve learning new information; others might involve rereading old information to complete a task.

Finally, it would be safe to assume that you still do not have a strategy for reading a second passage on thurboflyers, "How To Repair Malfunctioning Thurboflyers," because you still lack a schema for thurboflyers; you still have no purpose for reading, other than to memorize information to pass a test; and you will continue to encounter unknown technical terms and directions that are foreign to you. These observations are true even though you are presumably a mature, adult reader.

Implications of Reading as a Strategic Process for Learners Who Are Blind

The strategic process of reading is also applicable when the reader is blind and uses braille. The three factors—knowledge, purpose, and difficulty—apply to the braille reader. And although the braille reader must develop his or her own strategic processes to arrive at meaningful reading, the teacher plays a major role in helping the reader recognize and utilize appropriate strategies.

Much of this chapter has focused on the importance of knowledge. An important segment of knowledge is knowing the rules of the braille code. Many readers will learn the interactive and the psycholinguistic processes. The teacher must monitor knowledge of the code and intervene when needed.

The purposes of reading are not likely to be as broad for readers who are blind, simply because many materials may not be available in braille. The reading materials available to those who read print are extensive, including every item on the list just presented. Although the academic and recreational books and chapters on the list are likely to be available in braille, other items, such as recipes, may not be. Therefore, the teacher should encourage and motivate braille readers to cook using braille copies of recipes and even to braille their own written copies of the recipes. To broaden the purposes of reading for blind readers, teachers should place greater emphasis on reading materials that enhance daily living, such as the article from *Time* and even the IRS form. Those who use braille will have just as much difficulty reading the article about Thurboflyers as will those who use print, since both are limited in the extent to which the strategic process can result in meaningful reading.

Finally, the difficulty of the passage influences the need to use a strategic process. A good reader will be challenged by this difficulty, but a poor reader may lose the motivation to read and even develop a negative attitude about reading. If the teacher monitors the materials carefully and knows the students well, he or she can assist in their development of the technique of metacognition, which has been used successfully by both good readers and by students with learning disabilities.

DISCOVER YOUR PHILOSOPHY OF THE READING PROCESS

You have now been introduced to several points of view regarding the reading process. To discover your philosophy of the reading process within the context of teaching children who are blind, respond to the following statements.

Indicate your beliefs by circling one of the responses to the right of each statement: SA = strongly agree, A = agree, U = undecided, D = disagree, and SD = strongly disagree.

Integrated language process: Reading is one aspect of language that is closely related to the reader's writing, listening, and speaking abilities and experiences.   SA A U D SD

Developmental process: Reading is a visual-tactual language process that develops over time at different rates for different learners and is dependent on the learner's oral language development and experiential background.   SA A U D SD

Knowledge-based process: The ability to read involves the ability to comprehend meaning from specific knowledge-based (subject-matter) sources of information.   SA A U D SD

Social process: The ability to read is a necessary prerequisite for continued social development in the home, workplace, marketplace, and voting booth.   SA A U D SD

Cultural process: The ability to read is a necessary prerequisite for understanding our American cultural heritage, our multicultural roots, and the emerging global community.   SA A U D SD

Constructive, interactive process: Readers interact with text to construct meaning from text, based on their knowledge, background, and experiences (schema).   SA A U D SD

Psycholinguistic process: Readers use graphophonemic, syntactic, and semantic cues in deriving meaning from print.   SA A U D SD

Strategic (metacognitive) process: Readers adapt different reading strategies as they monitor their comprehension on the basis of their existing schema, their purpose in reading, and the difficulty of the text being read.   SA A U D SD

Affective process: Readers' ability to comprehend text is affected by their interests, attitudes, and motivation related to both reading and the nature of the materials being read.   SA A U D SD

Holistic process: Readers focus on comprehending whole text and whole language units by using their knowledge, background, and experiences to predict meaning.   SA A U D SD

Skills process: Readers focus on decoding printed symbols into words as the initial stage of comprehending word, sentence, paragraph, and whole-text units of meaning.   SA A U D SD

Interactive process: Readers use both their knowledge and decoding abilities to determine the meaning of the text.   SA A U D SD

WRITING

The previous section discussed one aspect of the communication process—reading. This section focuses on another aspect—writing. Writing actually begins the process of written communication when a writer prepares a message to be read later by another individual. The writer produces (or encodes) abstract written symbols that convey meaning to a defined audience, while the reader interprets (or decodes) the abstract symbols prepared by the writer. Meaningful literacy instruction during the school years assures that students will use writing and reading as effective communication tools. This section presents background information on writing. It begins with a working definition of writing that stands apart from any particular view of writing instruction. It then explores the role that abstract codes—print and braille—play in the written communication process, as well as the types or purposes of writing. Finally, it presents basic information on both the product and the process of writing.

Definition of Writing

Lindemann (1982, p. 11) defined writing as "a process of communication which uses a conventional graphic system to convey a message to a reader." She represented the relationship between the writer, the reader, and the message with the "communication triangle" illustrated in Figure 4-4. This triangle represents the various aspects of the communication process that occur in writing: a writer who conveys a written message to a reader and the subject (identified at the apex of the triangle), which is the more global subject matter from which the writer takes the specific message to be delivered.

Lindemann's definition of writing is equally applicable to writing in braille, although the conventional system used to convey the message is tactual (braille), rather than graphic (print). Foremost, writing in braille is a process of communication with the overriding goal of conveying a message to a defined audience. In this regard, individuals who are blind must be aware of, and address, the receptive written demands of the audience to whom they are communicating. For example, a student who is blind may send a memo in braille to a teacher of students with visual impairments requesting another volume in the mathematics book. Given that the special teacher has knowledge of braille, the memo will likely achieve its goal if it conforms to the conventions of standard English and the braille code. However, a similar memo to a librarian with no knowledge of braille likely would not be successful.

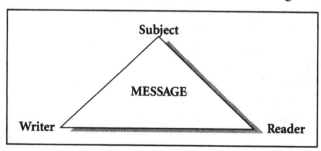

Figure 4-4. Lindemann's Communication Triangle. Source: *A Rhetoric for Writing Teachers* (p. 12), by E. Lindemann, 1982, New York: Oxford University Press. Copyright © 1982, Oxford University Press. Reprinted by permission.

It is incumbent on teachers of students with visual impairments to develop in their students a sense of the audiences to whom they are communicating and the requirements for the various receptive demands of those audiences. This process should begin early in a student's development of literacy skills. The accompanying suggestions will assist teachers in addressing audience demands.

Codes for Writing

Although it is not represented in Lindemann's communication triangle, the conventional graphic system, or code, is also an essential component of the writing process. The English graphic system contains (1) letters and conventions for arranging them into words and larger pieces of discourse; (2) a system of punctuation marks; and (3) mechanical customs, such as use of margins and indentations. As Lindemann (1982, p. 16) further explained:

SUGGESTIONS FOR DEVELOPING A SENSE OF AUDIENCE: RECEPTIVE COMMUNICATION DEMANDS

- Discuss with younger students the need to inkprint or interline assignments in braille before regular classroom teachers can grade their work.

- When a student plans to send a letter or greeting card, discuss whether the braille requires inkprinting. Also, using hand-over-hand guidance, if necessary, have the student sign his or her name in print when the reader to whom the letter or card is addressed uses print.

- Have the student make a list of significant adults and children in the school. Then identify whether each individual needs print or braille for reading.

- When discussing a writing task, have the student identify whether the audience reads in print or braille. If unsure of the needs of the audience, use print.

- In the late primary and early middle grades, begin to expand the student's repertoire of writing tools to include print media. Keyboarding skills and computer word processing are essential because they allow for direct communication with individuals who read print.

- Provide reinforcement when the student makes an appropriate choice of a written medium for a particular task. Provide constructive feedback when the student makes an inappropriate choice.

- As the student enters high school, transfer the primary responsibility for making decisions about all aspects of writing tasks to the student. Continue to provide constructive feedback on decisions that are made and continue to expand the student's repertoire of literacy tools.

- When helping the student develop this sense of audience, always focus on communicating meaning through writing. Remember to address other aspects of the writing task, such as the proper form for writing, the purpose for writing, and the content that will meaningfully communicate the intended purpose.

"Any code is both systematic and arbitrary. The alphabetic letters, punctuation marks, and mechanical customs of written English function together in predictable patterns, but the patterns are conventional. That is, we agree to use the symbols in certain ways." Thus, it is arbitrary that people who use English for communication identify a certain abstract shape as the letter *d*. It is also arbitrary that the combination of letters in *dog* represents a furry animal that barks. While arbitrary, our system of writing can be used for communication because English-speaking people agree on how specific symbols will be used and because we are systematic in their use. Without the systematic usage of a code, it would be impossible to communicate effectively.

Braille also has letters, along with two sets of conventions for arranging them into words and longer discourse—Lindemann's first characteristic of a written code. The first set of conventions in braille parallels the conventions of print. For example, words can be joined by hyphens to form hyphenated compound words, as in *merry-go-round*. The second set of conventions is specific to the braille code. The grade 2 braille code has a series of 189 contractions and short-form words, along with rules to govern them. The word *merry-go-round* would use not only the print conventions of hyphens to join the component parts, but the braille contractions *er*, *go*, and *ound*. In braille there is also a series of composition signs, such as capital and number signs, that have no inkprint counterparts.

Braille contains configurations for each of the punctuation marks in the graphic system—Lindemann's second characteristic of a written code. With recent changes in the rules governing the braille code, the use of punctuation marks almost always follows the practices of inkprint.

Braille also follows most mechanical customs of inkprint—Lindemann's third characteristic—but includes some unique customs. It uses indentations to identify paragraphs, but uses a two-cell indentation, rather than a half inch or five spaces. However, if paragraphs in inkprint were denoted by blank lines rather than by indentations, the braille system would eliminate the blank line and insert the standard two-cell indentation. Some other unique mechanical conventions of the braille system are the placement of inkprint and braille page numbers, the use of a dash at the beginning of a line, the division of words between pages, the inclusion of descriptions of pictures when appropriate, and the specific placement of headings.

Types of Writing

Writing for Different Purposes

There are a variety of different types of writing (or "modes of discourse"). Each serves a different purpose and, generally, a specific audience.

Writing assignments, especially in the elementary school, tend to emphasize expressive, narrative, or descriptive writing. *Expressive writing* allows the student to express him- or herself and is generally personal and not meant for others; the "audience" for this type of writing is oneself. *Narrative writing* is intended to "entertain by telling a story," and *descriptive writing* is intended to "present the details about a topic in a somewhat static context" (Noyce & Christie, 1989, p. 220). In using narration or description, the writer focuses on the message and on creating a message that can be appreciated in itself (Lindemann, 1982).

Other types of writing focus primarily on the reader or on "reality." *Persuasive writing* is intended to have a direct impact on a targeted audience for the purpose of persuading it to adopt a particular view; such writing is typically seen in debates and editorials (Lindemann, 1982). *Expository writing*, on the other hand, is intended to provide information (Sampson, Van Allen, & Sampson, 1991). Lindemann (1982) suggested that the primary focus of expository writing is on the reality or context; that is, this type of writing seeks to explain a body of knowledge or area of subject matter, such as science or geography. Noyce and Christie (1989, p. 221) stressed the importance of teaching children to develop expository writing skills, but suggested that it is a less familiar mode of discourse because children see so "few good models of expository writing in their reading materials and seldom engage in [the] production of expository text."

Calkins (1986, p. 14) suggested that there is a shift away from using modes of discourse to guide writing because "in real life there are no clear distinctions between modes"; rather, the process of writing should be stressed. However, two points are pertinent to this discussion of types of writing. First, it is necessary for children to see and use a wide variety of *forms* of discourse, such as letters, newspaper articles, textbooks, and poetry, to develop an essential knowledge of discourse. Second, it is important for those who are learning to write to select appropriate forms to complete the writing task. In this regard, Staab and Smith (1986) outlined various functions of writing and the possible forms or genres of each (see Table 4-1). Effective writing, though, is more than simply selecting a

Table 4-1. The Functions and Corresponding Forms (Genre) of Written Language

Function	*Possible Genre*
1. To entertain (primary purpose to provide enjoyment for self and others)	Stories, poetry, skits, dialogue, journals, notes, plays, jokes, letters
2. To inform (primary purpose to provide factual information)	Labels, lists, factual reports, logs, records, advertisements, invitations, programs, notes, dialogue journals
3. To control (primary purpose to direct the behaviors of self or others)	Signs, directions, recipes, notes, dialogue journals, invitations
4. To persuade (primary purpose to convince others)	Ads, stories, poetry, letters, notes
5. To communicate personal feelings (primary purpose to give a sense of the author's feelings)	Personal journals, dialogue journals, stories, poetry, skits, notes
6. To forecast, reason and evaluate (primary purpose stating of information plus justification)	Hypotheses, writing original story endings

Source: "Function in Written Language," by C. F. Staab and K. Smith, *English Quarterly, 19*, p. 53. Copyright © 1986, Canadian Council of Teachers of English Language Arts. Reprinted by permission.

form of discourse; as Lindemann (1982, p. 20) observed, "it involves making choices, posing questions, recording and reviewing possible solutions to a writing problem, and eventually, after many tentative formulations, creating the meaning we intended to convey to a reader about our subject."

Implications for Learners Who Are Blind

Children with normal vision obtain basic information on discourse or writing forms by observing writing being used all around them to accomplish specific functions. These incidental experiences are not available to the same extent for students who are blind. Therefore, teachers of students with visual impairments must ensure that blind students have access to a variety of forms of discourse in braille, such as signs, daily announcements, weekly school lunch menus, newspapers, magazines, and advertisements. Table 4-1 outlines some writing forms that should be made accessible to students who are blind. The special teacher prepares such forms in braille and other accessible media and then provides the student with direct exposure to the various forms of writing.

Although the types of writing tasks and the functions of writing are the same for all persons, regardless of the code they use, the way in which the writing task is accomplished may differ in some ways for individuals who use braille. As was mentioned earlier, a person who is blind must consider the receptive communication demands of the specific audience to which a message is being conveyed. Actually, this is only one part of addressing the demands of audience. With any writing task, the writer must do the following:

- Identify the purpose or function for writing.
- Consider the audience to which the message is being conveyed and ensure that the type or form of writing is appropriate (audience demand 1).
- Consider the receptive communication demands of the audience and ensure that an appropriate match is made in the receptive communication medium (audience demand 2).
- Complete the writing task, given the foregoing considerations, in a manner that will successfully convey the intended message.

Consider two illustrations of this process. First, a student who is blind is asked to keep a personal journal as a way of increasing his writing fluency and creativity. Given the personal (rather than public) demands of the writing task, the teacher makes sure that the student understands that this journal is strictly for the expression of feelings and is not intended to be read by others. Therefore, the student knows that the audience is himself. In considering the written medium to be used, he is free to choose whatever medium is most efficient for communicating with himself, so he chooses to write in braille. Finally, the student writes in a manner that will allow efficient rereading, but is not overconcerned with spelling, punctuation, and other conventions. He writes with enough accuracy to read back what he has written whenever he chooses.

Unfortunately, students often become confused by such personal writing tasks. Even though they are told that journals are for personal communication, teachers often respond by correcting misspellings, changing sentence structure, and providing suggestions. Such an intrusion in personal writing interferes with a student's development of the ownership of his or her writing. Routman (1991) suggested that if students choose to share their journals with teachers, only verbal feedback or removable notes should be provided. For students who use braille, a teacher's verbal response to the message being conveyed in journals is a valuable source of interaction between the student and teacher, whereas written feedback in braille provides a *model* for correct usage, rather than a listing of errors. By responding to the *content* of the message, the teacher shows the overriding value of the meaning being conveyed, rather than the specific component skills that are involved.

As a second illustration, consider a high school student who is blind who is requesting application materials for admission to college. The purpose of the writing task is stated clearly, so the student knows that a formal, concise letter is an appropriate type of writing. The audience for the writing task is a university staff person who likely will have a college degree, so the level and style of writing will be formal and professional. Considering the receptive written demands of the intended audience, the student knows that she must use print—a medium that is accessible to anyone. She also knows that letters on tape, while capable of effectively conveying the request, generally are considered inappropriate for such situations. Therefore, she chooses to create a concise business letter with a microcomputer word processor, review a braille copy, make needed revisions, edit the letter, and then output the final version in print. The student knows that the intended audience will expect perfection in writing, so there are no misspelled words or other gaps in the writing. In two weeks, she receives the information she requested. Given the planning that went into the writing task, it is to be expected that communication would be successful.

For teachers of students with visual impairments, the analysis of the demands of a writing task—often called the rhetorical demands—deserves special consideration in the development of literacy, since developing the twofold attention to audience demands is not likely to occur automatically. The need to consider the general audience demands is no different for students who are blind. However, as part of structuring writing tasks, the demands of the audience's receptive communication needs also must be addressed. The meaningful integration of both types of audience demands makes the completion of writing tasks successful for students who are blind.

THE WRITTEN PRODUCT

Apart from the process used to create a written product, several identifiable features are specific to the product itself. Isaacson (1984, p. 103) identified the following important components of writing, all of which are identifiable by outcome or product:

- fluency—the length of the paper
- syntactic maturity—the complexity of the sentences
- vocabulary—the use of a variety of words
- content—"organization of thought, originality, and style"

- conventions—"the mechanical aspects of writing, such as margins, grammar, spelling, and punctuation."

Some features of writing can be considered surface-level features, since they are directly observable from the paper. Surface-level features include penmanship, spelling, punctuation, capitalization, grammar, and syntax. Other features are not directly observable, but can be inferred from the product. Such higher-level features include content, organization, and style. The measurement of various features of the written product will be addressed in Chapter 7.

As was discussed in Chapter 3, braille is a code that can be used to convey English through writing. Since it is only a code, all the components of the written product just identified are present in braille, although some of the conventions may differ, such as the use of margins and indentation. Perhaps the most noticeable difference in written products is "penmanship"—a prominent feature of writing in print because there is an infinite number of possible penmanship styles, and students are often challenged to develop "acceptable" penmanship. In braille, there is one way to write characters, contractions, and words, and the observable product should always look the same. One may argue that students who are blind have much less difficulty developing the braille equivalent of penmanship than do students who use print.

The written product alone, despite its uniquely identifying features, does not reveal anything about the process the writer went through to create it. Many authorities (see, for example, Calkins, 1986; Graves, 1984; Routman, 1991) agree that an emphasis on written products overlooks most of the important aspects of writing. Because of the limited information provided in products, there has been a steady shift toward emphasizing writing as a process.

The Writing Process

The writing process has been defined as "everything a person does from the time he first contemplates the topic to the final moment when he completes the paper" (Graves, 1983, p. 250). A number of authors and researchers have proposed and named various elements of the writing process. For example, Graves (1984) identified three elements—precomposing, composing, and postcomposing—and Yatvin (1981) suggested four phases: exploring, composing, editing, and going public. Regardless of the number of phases or elements, each focuses on the *process* that is used to create a final manuscript or product.

Elements in the Process

The five elements in the writing process described by Leu and Kinzer (1991)—prewriting, drafting, revision, editing, and publishing—are summarized in Table 4-2. Leu and Kinzer (p. 346) stated that "*prewriting* experiences are designed to generate potential topics and writing ideas by helping students explore either personal knowledge or new information that is related to their writing task." Routman (1991, p. 164) prefers the term *percolating*, since it represents "the ongoing, thinking, reconsidering process that takes place throughout the writing process."

Drafting, the next phase in the writing process "consists of initial attempts to capture ideas in writing" (Leu & Kinzer, 1991, p. 347). The goal here is to get ideas down on paper, not to focus on spelling, grammar, conventions, and so forth. Calkins (1986, p. 17) likes the term *drafting*, since "it implies the tentativeness of our early efforts. Like an artist with a sketch pad, we begin to find the contours of our subject. We make light, quick lines; nothing is permanent."

Revising involves rereading a paper, considering what has been written, and then making changes in the *content* of the paper (Leu & Kinzer, 1991). Revision is not to be confused with correcting spelling, punctuation, and other errors—that phase occurs next. Revision focuses on changes in the content of the paper and may even (and often does) involve returning to earlier phases in the writing process. "Revision means, literally, looking again at a piece of writing and *re*-visioning it" (Routman, 1991, p. 165).

Editing occurs near the end of the writing process and focuses on changes to the "surface characteristics of writing, including spelling, capitalization, punctuation, and usage" (Leu & Kinzer, 1991, p. 349). Sampson et al. (1991, p. 94) cautioned teachers to keep editing in its proper perspective: "If we begin too early to stress the mechanical and formal elements of writing or if we stress them at the expense of the quality of thought communicated, we may create a distaste for writing....Correct form must serve—never rule—writing." In a meaning-centered approach to teaching writing, it is at this phase in the writing process that spelling and other conventions are taught.

Another element in the writing process, generally the final one, is *publishing*, which involves sharing one's writing with a wider audience (Leu & Kinzer, 1991). It may take the form of publishing in a bound book, displaying on a bulletin board, printing in a school newspaper, or sharing during a schoolwide author's day. Yatvin (1981, p. 52) suggested that this "going public" phase is a "construction step rather than a writing step." Writing that is intended for audiences other than the self—public writing—is published. Therefore, not all writing of children will be published, since some of it is not intended for a wider audience. Private writing, as defined by Yatvin, is intended to be read by oneself or close acquaintances and is not intended to be scrutinized for neatness or correctness; therefore, publishing such creations would not be appropriate.

Table 4-2. Elements in the Writing Process

Element	*Purpose*
Prewriting	To generate topics and ideas for writing activities.
Drafting	To write down initial ideas and thoughts on paper.
Revising	To make content changes in the paper.
Editing	To make corrections in spelling, capitalization, usage, and so on.
Publishing	To prepare one's writing to be shared with a wider audience.

Source: Based on concepts from *Effective Reading Instruction, K-8*, 2nd ed., by D. J. Leu and C. K. Kinzer, 1991, New York: Merrill.

On the surface, the writing process appears linear in form; it starts with prewriting activities and ends with publishing. Such is not the case, however, as Calkins (1986, p. 18) illustrated:

> The shifts between rehearsal [prewriting], drafting, revision, and editing occur minute by minute, second by second, throughout the writing process. The writer thinks of a topic, jots down a few lines, rereads them. Dissatisfied, the writer may cross out a line and recopy the remaining text, making small changes. The piece still looks feeble. Trying again, the writer asks, "What do I want to say?" and this time, jots down some notes. They are messy, so the writer recopies them. Already the writer has shifted from rehearsal to drafting, to revision, to editing, to rehearsal, to editing.

In addition to noting the recursive (versus linear) nature of the writing process, Leu and Kinzer (1991) indicated that it is not necessary for students to complete each phase in the writing process for everything they write. Some writing tasks, such as journal writing, are not likely to be edited or published. The key is to focus on the purpose of the writing task and to ensure that the necessary elements of the writing process are used to achieve that purpose.

Implications of the Process of Writing in Braille

A critical analysis of the elements in the writing process suggests that differences likely exist when writing in braille. Writing with a braillewriter is less flexible and less "recursive" than is writing in print. Both the revision and editing of a paper are more cumbersome with a brailler, and feedback from a regular classroom teacher is less readily accessible to the student. Some possible concerns in the writing process for students who are blind are listed in

Table 4-3. Possible Areas of Concern in Each Element in the Writing Process for Students Who Are Blind

Element	Possible Areas of Concern
Prewriting	• Possible restrictions on the range and variety of background experiences needed for assuring that writing is meaningful.
	• Less access to others with similar experiences to explore ideas for writing.
Drafting	• Restrictions in feedback from the teacher as the initial draft is being written.
	• Possible slowness of writing with a braillewriter.
Revising	• Restrictions in making global revisions in a paper, such as moving, adding, or deleting large blocks of text, without the need to recopy the entire paper.
	• A greater willingness to accept the first draft as the final product because of the cumbersomeness of recopying the paper.
Editing	• The difficulty in doing the final editing without recopying the paper.
	• The lack of assistance from the regular classroom teacher in editing.
	• The need to wait for the special teacher to assist in editing.
Publishing	• The need to make writing accessible to appropriate audiences that generally read print.

Table 4-3. It is noteworthy, however, that accessible word processing and other technology will minimize or eliminate most of these concerns and will greatly facilitate the writing process, as discussed in Chapter 6.

Relatively little is known about the writing process of persons who are blind. However, there is some initial evidence that although some differences exist, the process of writing in braille is similar to the process of writing in print (Bryant, 1985; Lyenberger-Pfohl, 1988). These findings indicate that persons who are blind incorporate the various elements of the writing process—prewriting, drafting, revising, editing, and publishing—when writing in braille.

However, when 13 year olds and 17 year olds were asked in a questionnaire about their writing, fewer students who were blind reported writing a paper more than once before turning it in than their age mates with normal vision (Koenig, 1988); this finding suggests that students who are blind pay less attention to the revision and editing elements of the process. Also, fewer blind 13 year olds reported being encouraged to jot down ideas or to make outlines before writing, which suggests that less attention is paid to prewriting activities.

Differences also were documented in the ways in which teachers of students with visual impairments responded to their students' writing. Most 13 and 17 year olds who were blind reported that their teachers "usually" discussed a paper with them when it was returned, whereas most sighted students reported that their teachers "sometimes" discussed a paper when it was returned (Koenig, 1988). It is unclear whether this finding represents an advantage for students who were blind, a disadvantage, or both. Clearly, appropriate, timely feedback from teachers is essential in fostering growth in writing. If special teachers provide feedback on the content of the writing to help the students with their revisions, a qualitative advantage would exist. If special teachers provide feedback on errors in writing *after* the revision process, students would have information they needed to "clean up" their writing, but would not have a written model in braille to assist them at this point in the writing process. Ideally, both sources of feedback—verbal and written—should be provided *throughout all phases* of the writing process. Feedback should not be confined to only a few elements of the process.

The limited information available on the writing process of persons who are blind and write in braille suggests that this process is both similar to and different from the process used by persons with normal vision who write in print. Special teachers will facilitate the writing process by appreciating and attending to both the similarities and differences. Strategies for supporting the writing process for students who are blind are presented in Chapter 6.

SUMMARY

Reading is a constructive, interactive, and strategic process that is based on the reader's knowledge, background, and prior experience. To ensure that children who are blind are prepared to bring meaning to what they read, they need a rich schemata to provide the basis for literacy learning. Implementing the five basic principles of special methods for teaching children who are blind—individualization, concreteness, unified instruction, additional stimulation, and self-activity—helps to ensure the development of quality experiences, language, and concepts.

Writing by braille is a process of communicating a message to an intended audience using a conventional tactual system. Although the process differs from writing in print largely on the basis of the code used for writing, there are more substantive differences in writing by braille that influence the instructional process. Special teachers must provide their students with direct opportunities to observe a variety of writing forms in accessible media. Also, students must learn to recognize and address the receptive communication demands of audiences to whom they are communicating. To use writing for effective communication, students must use all elements of the writing process to ensure that their intended message is conveyed meaningfully to their intended audience.

Reading and writing are both part of a holistic language process and therefore should be integrated into literacy instruction. The same schema that makes reading meaningful to a literacy learner also makes writing meaningful, as well as speaking and listening. When the special teacher takes the needed time to expand and enrich the background experiences of a child who is blind, the teacher is building the foundation for literacy and life skills. Chapters 5 and 6 explore various approaches and strategies for teaching reading and writing, respectively, focusing on the development of meaningful literacy skills.

REFERENCES

Anderson, R. C., Hiebert, E. H., Scott, J. A., & Wilkinson, I. A. G. (1985). *Becoming a nation of readers: The report of the Commission on Reading.* Washington, DC: National Academy of Education, National Institute of Education.

Baker, R., & Shaw-Baker, M. (1992, July). *Implementing holistic literacy strategies in Chinese teacher preparation programs.* Paper presented at the International Reading Association 14th World Congress on Reading, Maui, HI.

Barraga, N. (1986). Sensory perceptual development. In G. T. Scholl (Ed.), *Foundations of education for blind and visually impaired children and youth.* New York: American Foundation for the Blind.

Blos, J. W. (1974). Traditional rhymes and games: Language learning experiences for pre-school blind children. *New Outlook for the Blind, 68,* 268-275.

Bryant, D. G. (1985). The composing processes of blind writers (Doctoral dissertation, North Texas State University, 1984). *Dissertation Abstracts International, 45,* 3296A.

Calkins, L. M. (1986). *The art of teaching writing.* Portsmouth, NH: Heinemann Educational Books.

Cromer, R. F. (1983). The implication of research findings on blind children for semantic theories and for intervention programmes. In A. E. Mills (Ed.), *Language acquisition in the blind child.* San Diego: College Hills Press.

Erin, J. (1986). Frequencies and types of questions in the language of visually impaired children. *Journal of Visual Impairment & Blindness, 80,* 670-764.

Ferrell, K. A. (1985). *Reach out and teach.* New York: American Foundation for the Blind.

Goodman, K. S. (1976a). The reading process: A psycholinguistic view. In Smith, E. B., Goodman, K. S., and Meredith, R. (Eds.), *Language and thinking in schools* (2nd ed.). New York: Holt, Rinehart & Winston.

Goodman, K. S. (1976b). Reading: A psycholinguistic guessing game. In H. Singer & R. Ruddell (Eds.), *Theoretical models and processes of reading* (2nd ed.). Newark, DE: International Reading Association.

Graves, D. H. (1983). *Writing: Teachers and children at work.* Portsmouth, NH: Heinemann.

Graves, D. H. (1984). *A researcher learns to write: Selected articles and monographs.* Portsmouth, NH: Heinemann.

Henderson, F. M. (1960). Little bumps that say something. *Exceptional Children, 26,* 261-266.

Henderson, F. M. (1973). Communication skills. In B. Lowenfeld (Ed.), *The visually handicapped child in school* (pp. 218-229). New York: John Day.

Isaacson, S. (1984). Evaluating written expression: Issues of reliability, validity, and instructional utility. *Diagnostique, 9,* 96–116.

Koenig, A. J. (1988). A study of expressive writing skills of blind students including partial replication of the National Assessment of Educational Progress third writing evaluation (Doctoral dissertation, Vanderbilt University, 1987). *Dissertation Abstracts International, 48,* 1734A.

Leu, D. J., & Kinzer, C. K. (1991). *Effective reading instruction, K-8* (2nd ed.). New York: Merrill.

Lindemann, E. (1982). *A rhetoric for writing teachers.* New York: Oxford University Press.

Lowenfeld, B. (Ed.). (1973). *The visually handicapped child in school.* New York: John Day.

Lowenfeld, B. (1980). Psychological problems of children with severely impaired vision. In W. M. Cruickshank (Ed.), *Psychology of exceptional children and youth* (4th ed.). Englewood Cliffs, NJ: Prentice-Hall.

Lowenfeld, B. (1981). Effects of blindness on the cognitive functions of children. In B. Lowenfeld (1981), *Berthold Lowenfeld on blindness and blind people. Selected papers* (pp. 67-78). New York: American Foundation for the Blind). (Original work published in 1948.)

Lyenberger-Pfohl, E. M. (1988). A case study of the composing processes of two congenitally blind students. (Doctoral dissertation, Indiana University of Pennsylvania, 1987). *Dissertation Abstracts International, 48,* 3089A–3090A.

Miller, D. D. (1985). Reading comes naturally: A mother and her blind child's experiences. *Journal of Visual Impairment & Blindness, 79,* 1-4.

Mills, A. E. (1983a). Acquisition of speech sounds in the visually handicapped child. In A. E. Mills (Ed.), *Language acquisition in the blind child.* San Diego: College Hills Press.

Mills, A. E. (Ed.). (1983b). *Language acquisition in the blind child.* San Diego: College Hills Press.

Noyce, R. M., & Christie, J. F. (1989). *Integrating reading and writing instruction in grades K-8.* Boston: Allyn & Bacon.

Rex, E. J. (1989). Issues related to literacy of legally blind learners. *Journal of Visual Impairment & Blindness, 83,* 306-313.

Rogow, S. M. (1988). *Helping the visually impaired child with developmental problems.* New York: Teachers College Press.

Routman, R. (1991). *Invitations: Changing as teachers and learners K–12.* Portsmouth, NH: Heinemann.

Sampson, M., Van Allen, R., & Sampson, M. B. (1991). *Pathways to literacy.* Fort Worth: Holt, Rinehart, & Winston.

Smith, F. (1978). *Reading without nonsense.* New York: Teachers College Press.

Smith, F. (1976) *Understanding reading.* New York: Holt, Rinehart & Winston.

Staab, C. F., & Smith, K. (1986). Function in written language. *English Quarterly, 19,* 50-57.

Stephens, B., & Grube, C. (1982). Development of Piagetian reasoning in congenitally blind children. *Journal of Visual Impairment & Blindness, 76,* 133-143.

Stratton, J. M., & Wright, S. (1991). On the way to literacy: Early experiences for young visually handicapped students. *RE:view, 23,* 55-62.

Swenson, A. M. (1988). Using an integrated literacy curriculum with beginning braille readers. *Journal of Visual Impairment & Blindness, 82,* 336-338.

Yatvin, J. (1981). A functional writing program for the middle grades. In S. Haley-James (Ed.), *Perspectives on writing in grades 1–8* (pp. 43–57). Urbana, IL: National Council of Teachers of English.

BRAILLE READING LITERACY: APPROACHES AND STRATEGIES

Controversy over the most effective instructional approaches and strategies for teaching reading has existed for well over 25 years. Frequently, the different points of view have been heightened and reinforced by advocates of either extreme skills-centered philosophies or extreme holistic meaning-centered philosophies. Recently, "middle of the road," interactive philosophies have emerged to fit the realities of classroom instruction and learning (Leu & Kinzer, 1991; Reutzel & Cooter, 1992; Vacca, Vacca, & Gove, 1991).

MODELS OF READING INSTRUCTION

Theoretical models of instruction have been developed to focus on the differing points of view regarding the reading process. These models, graphically portrayed in most reading texts (Vacca, Vacca, & Gove, 1991; Weaver, 1994), are then translated into approaches for instruction; and the approaches evolve into specific teaching strategies. The theoretical models are presented here first as background for the discussion of approaches and strategies, followed by implications for the use of these models when the learner is blind and reads by braille.

Meaning-Centered Models

Meaning-centered models of instruction focus on the reader's knowledge and experience to predict or determine meaning from print or braille (see Figure 5-1). The overriding emphasis is placed on deriving meaning from text.

One example of such a model is Goodman's (1976) psycholinguistic model of reading instruction. According to Goodman, meaning focuses on comprehending whole language units—whole text. Readers use their knowledge of semantic, syntactic, and graphophonic relationships (cues) to predict the meaning of text and subsequently to confirm or reject their predictions. Good-man referred to this reading process as a "psycholinguistic guessing game" in which readers constantly predict, confirm, or reject hypotheses related to the meaning of whole language units, not of their discrete parts.

Skills-Centered Models

Skills-centered models of reading instruction focus on decoding print symbols into words as the initial stage of the reading process (see Figure 5-2). Instruction emphasizes the component skills in reading. Proponents of these models assert that learning graphophonemic relationships initially allows readers to decode words, which, in turn, allows them to comprehend the meaning of sentences, paragraphs, and whole text units of written language. The initial emphasis is on decoding visual-tactual information into words to gain meaning.

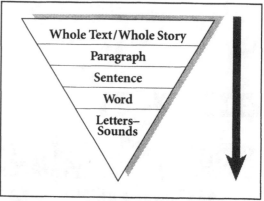

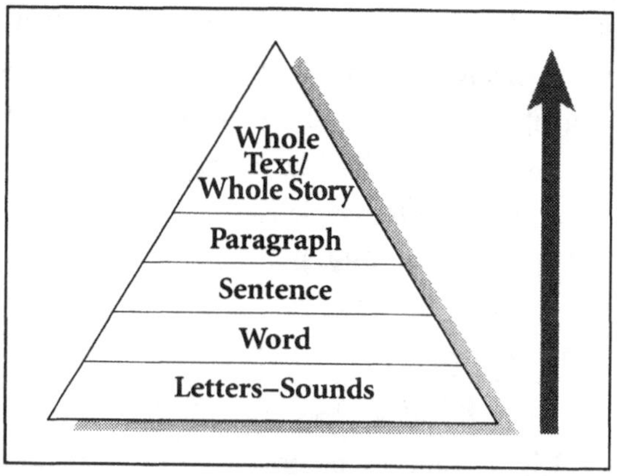

Figure 5-1. The Meaning-Based Model of Reading Instruction

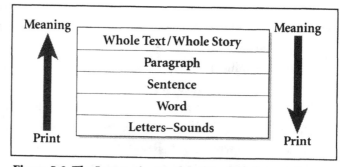

Figure 5-2. The Skills-Based Model of Reading Instruction

Interactive Models

Interactive models of reading instruction propose an intermediate position and suggest that neither knowledge nor graphophonemic information is used exclusively by readers (Vacca, Vacca, & Gove, 1991). Readers who have a well-developed schema (knowledge, background, and experience) make minimal use of graphophonemic cues to confirm hypotheses while reading, whereas readers who do not have appropriate schema tend to focus more on the printed information to gain meaning (see Figure 5-3).

Within the context of this chapter, the term *approaches* refers to broadly based instructional approaches, such as the basal reader approach, language experience approach, literature-based approach, and whole language approach, which are described later.

Figure 5-3. The Interactive Model of Reading Instruction

Strategies refer to specific instructional methods, activities, and materials that are used with one or several approaches to teaching reading.

Implications of Three Models of Instruction for Learners Who Are Blind

The three models just introduced are currently being used by reading teachers of children who are blind. Some are regular education teachers in whose classroom the children are included on a part-time or full-time basis. Other teachers have had special training to work with blind children. The two types of teachers function as a team, each bringing special competencies to the reading instruction of their students who are blind.

Teachers select the model of instruction to be used based on their philosophies of reading instruction or on the materials that are available to them. Often, models and materials are chosen by the school district.

All three models have been used to provide reading instruction to learners who are blind, but no research has been done to show which is the most efficient model. In the past, the skills-centered model was used extensively with children who were blind (Lowenfeld, Abel, & Hatlen, 1969), probably because of the nature of the braille code, the limitations of the tactual perceptual unit, and the practices of the time. In the past 25 years, however, reading instruction has moved from the skills-centered model to the meaning-centered model or the interactive model as a result of these children's increasing inclusion in regular classrooms.

The interactive model allows the teacher to choose activities from the more meaning-centered point on the continuum if the child has well-developed language and concepts and has had a wide range of experiences. It also allows the teachers to choose activities toward the skills-centered point on the continuum if the child is not learning needed skills as he or she uses meaning-centered activities.

Although teachers are the key to the implementation of any model, a model should be chosen on the basis of the attributes and needs of the child who is blind and reads braille. The high-functioning child with a well-developed schema should have the opportunity to work at the meaning-centered level, developing skills through his or her own inferences. The lower-functioning child should be provided with experiences to develop a schema, as well as instruction to develop skills that do not come as readily to the child as to some of his or her peers. Considerations related to the three models will be presented throughout the discussions of various approaches and strategies.

INSTRUCTIONAL APPROACHES

In the early 1960s, the U.S. Office of Education funded the "First Grade Studies"—a series of 27 research studies designed to determine the most effective approaches for teaching beginning reading. In short, these studies concluded that (1) there is *no best method* for teaching beginning reading and (2) the *classroom teacher* is the most important variable in determining effective reading instruction (Bond & Dykstra, 1967). These findings are worth remembering as we consider several ongoing current debates, such as skills-centered versus meaning-centered instruction; basal readers versus whole language; phonics versus sight words; and language experience versus whole language.

More recently, *Becoming a Nation of Readers* (Anderson, Hiebert, Scott, & Wilkinson, 1985) suggested the following changes in classroom instruction:

- Teachers should devote more time to comprehension instruction.
- Teachers should spend less time completing workbooks and skill sheets.
- Children should spend more time in independent reading.
- Children should spend more time writing.
- Teachers of beginning reading should present well-designed phonics instruction. Instruction should be kept simple and should be completed by the end of second grade for most children.

Within the context of these findings, this section presents an overview of four instructional approaches involving basal readers, language experience, literature, and whole language, as well as the implications of each approach for teaching blind children. As you read each description, consider where you would place each instructional approach on the continuum in Figure 5-4.

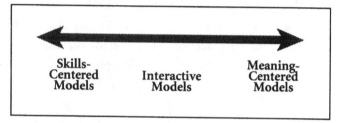

Figure 5-4. Continuum of Models

Basal Reader Approach

According to Flood and Lapp (1986), basal readers are used in 92 to 98 percent of today's elementary schools. Total basal reader programs consist of a sequentially arranged series of reading textbooks, workbooks, teachers' guides, scope and sequence charts of reading skills, tests, and supplemental workbook and practice materials (Mason & Au, 1990). The basal reader series begin with texts for kindergarten or first grade and usually continue through the sixth-grade level. The texts are intended for use in daily instructional sessions, usually with small groups of learners. The teacher uses a teacher's guide that provides comprehensive information on how to present each lesson, with suggestions for activities to prepare the learner for new reading competencies or to strengthen competencies that have already been taught.

Instruction tends to be teacher directed within the context of the format of the directed reading activity (DRA) lesson plan that consists of (1) preview and preparation information and activities, (2) guided oral and silent reading practice, (3) skill development and practice, and (4) extension activities and enrichment (Leu & Kinzer, 1991). Specific skills to be taught within the scope and sequence of the series are categorized under broad skills areas, such as word-recognition skills, vocabulary skills, comprehension skills, study skills, and literature skills. The text of the basal readers follows this guide closely. Most basal reader texts assess the learner's progress through curriculum-based assessment techniques or through criterion-referenced tests at key points, usually when the learner is ready to move from one book to another.

The basal reader approach usually corresponds to the skills-centered model (Weaver, 1994) of instruction. Early instruction concentrates on the basic graphophonemic (letter-sound relationships) aspects of language, with an emphasis on sight words-whole words that can be recognized easily in a single visual fixation. The learner then uses his or her knowledge of letter-sound relationships and store of sight words to recognize new words. The two- and three-word sentences that are introduced early in the materials are not usually very meaningful and tend to focus on letter-sound relationships for recognition. Even so, the teacher can use these short sentences to help the learner develop and utilize syntactical (grammatical) skills. It is also hoped that the materials and the teacher will soon direct the learner to use semantic skills to recognize words through their anticipated meanings.

In most basal reader series, the emphasis on letter-sound relationships and the rules related to their use continue as the reader progresses into the middle grades. Gradually, the focus shifts to longer sentences in which syntax and semantics are stressed, along with the sentence, rather than individual letters and words. Eventually, the learner reaches the top of the model, and the emphasis is on the whole story. Several of the basal reader series are moving toward the interactive model, with the expectation that the reader will also develop competency to construct meaning from stories.

Implications of the Basal Reader Approach for Learners Who Are Blind

Role of Teachers

In the basal reader and other instructional approaches, teachers play similar roles. The special teacher keeps the regular teacher alert to the blind child's special needs, and the regular teacher keeps the special teacher alert to the blind child's problems in reading the same materials as his or her classmates. For example, the two-line, or runover, sentence is (usually) introduced at the point in the sequence of skills at which the sighted child is judged to be ready. Since more space is usually needed to write the same passage in braille, the blind child is almost certain to encounter a runover sentence before his or her peers do so. The special teacher can monitor the child's reading materials to determine when this skill must be introduced to the child who reads braille. The regular teacher should be informed and can introduce the skill, probably in a brief individual session prior to the group reading session. The two teachers work together closely to meet the blind child's needs and to solve his or her problems. Obviously, such a program requires teamwork and daily conferences between the two teachers.

An important role of the special teacher in either of the approaches, or various settings, is to monitor the child's learning of the braille code. The teacher will be competent in reading and writing braille and will introduce the elements of the braille code. However, the code need not, and should not, be introduced as a separate skill or competency, but should be introduced within the context of meaningful literacy experiences. Learning of the braille code may take place in an inductive fashion as the learner engages in reading and writing experiences. If inductive learning is not taking place, specific strategies can be utilized to provide some deductive experiences and to strengthen inductive learning. The solution should not be to rely on skills-centered experiences. Isolated drill and practice in the various elements of the code, its signs, and its rules will not motivate the child to enjoy reading and learning to read. The solution, rather, is to help the child grow through interactive or meaning-centered experiences. Knowledge of the braille code is part of the reader's schema. As that component of schema develops, comprehension, speed, motivation, attitude, and self-esteem will also develop.

The regular teacher also plays a role in the child's progress in knowledge and use of the code. He or she will provide meaningful experiences in both areas of literacy—reading and writing. As noted, the teachers work closely with one another, functioning as a team and sharing information about the child's needs and progress.

Transliterated Braille Texts

In an inclusive program, as well as in other settings, blind children use braille editions of the same basal reader series their peers are using. If a basal reader series is to be the major text and if the child is able to progress satisfactorily and keep up with his or her sighted peers, transliterated text is recommended. There are several limitations to the use of such texts, however, particularly during the emergent literacy stage. First, because basal readers at this early stage depend heavily on pictures rather than on words for meaning, the child with little or no vision misses this presentation of the story's meaning. Second, the words and language in the print edition are selected with no consideration of the unique attributes of the braille code. For example, difficult multiple-cell signs appear early on. Third, the content of the stories does not consider the limited experiences of the blind learner. Fourth, at the higher level, the language and the braille code are increasingly inconsistent. Concern for the use of print to braille transliterations has been reported by Rex (1970, 1971) and Bleiberg (1970). The best learning environment for the use of a transliterated text when using a basal reader approach appears to be a resource room or daily visits by the itinerant teacher to the child in an integrated classroom. The residential setting does not present the same problems with the basal reader approach.

Other Concerns About Transliterated Texts

Not all basal reader series are available in braille. Although APH does publish the braille edition of several series, there are some problems in this process. First, it is not possible for one publisher to reproduce in braille all the work of other publishers. Second, it has been equally impossible to produce a revised braille edition of a basal reader series until the print version has been completed. For a year or longer following revision, the blind child may be reading an older edition. If the revision is radical, the blind child may not be able to use the same series. Such problems may soon be alleviated, as APH (and individual states through legislation known as "braille bills") is working with textbook publishers to provide computer disks as books, original or revised, are published.

Patterns: The Primary Braille Reading Program

Motivated by such concerns as the limitations of transliterated texts and the frequent lack of availability, in 1975 APH initiated the development of a beginning braille reading series, eventually to be called *Patterns: The Primary Braille Reading Program* (Caton, Pester, & Bradley, 1980). *Patterns* is composed of the texts, worksheets, teacher's guides, and criterion-referenced tests common to most basal reader series of the late 1970s and early 1980s. The final text is at the third reader level (*not* necessarily commensurate with the third grade). By the end of fourth grade, the learner is prepared to read from the texts used by his or her sighted peers.

Early in the development of *Patterns*, a set of research-based specifications for the selection and sequencing of vocabulary, as well as the content of the stories, was designated (Caton, 1979). An eclectic, "strong experience approach was selected . . . with certain phonological and syntactical notions added as students progressed through the various levels. Such linguistic learnings were sequenced in light of the special characteristics of the braille code" (Caton & Bradley, 1978–79, p. 69).

The *Patterns* texts are used extensively in both day school and residential school programs. If the reading program in the regular class uses basal readers as the major instructional text, *Patterns* is often chosen as the blind child's braille text. Its use as the major text implies the need for daily sessions with the special teacher. In day school programs, it also implies that there are large blocks of time in which the blind child is not likely to be included with his sighted peers and thus may miss out on opportunities to further his or her language-communication skills and to share experiences. If this separation from sighted peers is the only way that a blind child can achieve literacy, then it must be done. However, it is hoped that the blind child will be included in as many nontext language and communication activities as possible, both academic and otherwise.

The decision to use *Patterns* depends on a number of factors. If a basal reader series is the instructional approach, the teacher may limit herself or himself to that approach. Essentially, *Patterns* uses a skills-centered model of reading instruction. However, *Patterns* can also be used appropriately as a component of the interactive model. It can be used with other types of text, such as language-experience-generated text, stories, "big books," and trade books. Selected stories and activities from *Patterns* will be especially meaningful; some stories relate to the learner's blindness, such as the story of Ping, the braille writer, in an early level and the story of Louis Braille in an upper level. *The Patterns Library Series* supplements *Patterns*, reinforcing skills and introducing experiences. *Patterns: The Primary Spelling and English Program* has been developed by APH to accompany the basal reader series and encourage the integrated language process.

If the teacher or school in which the blind child is enrolled is whole language oriented, a basal reader will not be the text of choice. Again, however, portions of *Patterns* may serve as augmentative text. The teacher can use its many suggested activities to ensure that the braille code, with its many rules, is presented in sequential stages of difficulty, enhanced by reading passages that reinforce the rules in a way that transliterated braille texts do not. In a sense, *Patterns* selections can become the literature of the meaning-centered model of instruction. Stories at the higher levels are adapted versions of well-known literature, and poems are frequently used.

The scenario presented in Chapter 4 showed how Tim, a child who is blind, and Ms. Blakey, his itinerant teacher, used *Patterns* to enhance the reading activities he shared with his peers in the regular class. Neither of Tim's teachers would choose the skills-centered model for reading instruction, but *Patterns* has a role in Tim's learning to read. Its contents should not be ignored because of its format. Some of its contents are a means to literacy at several stages—early literacy, emergent literacy, and extended literacy. Its focus on the special code that blind children read makes portions of it a primary means to braille literacy.

The teacher is the key in reading instruction, not the text. The good teacher will use *Patterns* and any other text judiciously as she or he provides instruction and opportunities for the blind child to read by braille as reading becomes a constructive interactive process by which meaning is derived.

Language Experience Approach

The language experience approach focuses on the use of children's oral language and real-life experiences as the basis for creating personalized reading materials (Mason & Au, 1990). Reading begins with a familiar and meaningful story, composed by the readers and utilizing familiar words in a syntactical form that is familiar to them. This approach was one of the first to integrate writing and reading experiences. It is widely used today.

Leu and Kinzer (1991) listed four procedural steps that teachers follow when using a language experience approach:

1. Give children a vivid experience that provides the content for the story.
2. Elicit oral language from students that describes the experience.
3. Transcribe the students' oral language on a chalkboard or an experience chart.
4. Help students read what was transcribed.

Implications of the Language Experience Approach for Learners Who Are Blind

You were introduced to the language experience approach earlier when you met Tim, his teachers, and his peers in Chapter 4. In the scenario "Tim is Learning to Read and Write," Tim was part of a group, but he and Ms. Blakey could develop texts without other children or teachers. And, although Tim might have written one-word or one-sentence stories earlier in the year, his stories are likely to become longer as he progresses in this approach to learning to read. The length of his stories will be determined by the complexity and number of sentences, both of which are an outgrowth of Tim's oral language and developing schema for writing. This approach ensures that Tim has a sufficient schema for reading his own story.

One advantage of the language experience approach is that the teacher actually writes the story on the braillewriter as Tim dictates to her. If a computer and other appropriate software and technology are available, Ms. Blakey or an aide can write as Tim dictates and immediately provide a hard copy for his use. It is assumed that the adult who does the mechanical writing has the competence in braille writing to provide an accurate copy. Tim then has a model braille copy of his story and a tangible example that reading is speech written down.

Tim may read language experience stories individually or with a group. Depending on his needs in constructing meaningful reading, the teacher can focus on graphophonic skills, semantic skills, or syntactical skills. She and Tim can use the redundancy of the letters, words, and grammar to help him read the story at a faster rate, and comprehend its meaning just as well. The language experience text will also give Tim the opportunity to make inferences and use rules of the braille code.

This approach is flexible. It is used primarily by teachers who espouse the holistic (whole language) view of reading instruction, but it is also used by teachers who prefer a more skills-centered view.

The language experience approach may be used to enhance the basal reader series or individual texts, such as trade books. Furthermore, it is as effective in a residential school setting as in a public school setting. However, as in any approach, teachers are the key factor in instruction. If they do not accept the child's writing, the child loses the sense of motivation and purpose.

Literature-Based Approach

Interesting and challenging children's literature—both narrative and expository—provides the foundation for literature-based approaches in a variety of classroom settings. The focus is on meaning, interpretation, and enjoyment. Literature-based reading instruction can take several forms, including the use of self-selected core books with an entire class, individualized self-selected books for study, and integrated or thematic units of instruction using a wide variety of trade books and children's literature organized around a central theme (Reutzel & Cooter, 1992).

Literature-based instructional strategies include a variety of reading and writing activities: independent reading through sustained silent reading (SSR), individual conferences with teachers, cooperative learning groups, language experience approach activities, literature response projects, literature response journal writing, book talks, story maps, literature theme units, and readers' workshops. Skills are taught within the context of literature study, as needed. Typically, teachers address the development of skills through mini-lessons or individual conferences with students.

Implications of the Literature-Based Approach for Learners Who Are Blind

The literature-based approach lies between the interactive and the meaning-centered model of instruction, and its roots are in the old individualized reading approach. "The individualized format...is based on sound principles and offers ideas that can be used to supplement any reading program" (Harley, Truan, & Sanford, 1987, p. 55). The literature-based, individualized text can be used with braille readers to enhance the basal reader approach or the language experience approach, or it may be used successfully as the total instructional approach.

There are several advantages to the literature-based approach. First, the children read topics that are interesting to them and thus are more likely to bring the necessary schema to the text. Second, children can read at their own rate and level of comprehension and use a personal reading-learning style, global or analytic. Third, in most classrooms that use the literature-based approach, readers can choose when and where in the room they want to read (Carbo, Dunn, & Dunn, 1986). Because readers read what, where, when, and how they want to read, they are likely to understand why they read.

The literature-based approach has a number of limitations in its use with children who are blind. Obviously, such an individualized approach is demanding of the teacher's time. If the group is large, learners may not receive sufficient attention from the teachers to develop their individual literacy. The regular classroom teacher may not be competent to monitor the child who is reading braille texts, and the itinerant teacher may not be present when the child is reading. If a resource-room teacher is in the building or if the itinerant teacher can be in the classroom for large blocks of time, it would seem feasible to use a literature-based approach for at least part of the instructional time.

The literature-based approach also requires a large supply of books that span a wide range of reading levels and topics and are located in or near the classroom. Unfortunately, even if books from all available resources (such as state materials depositories and Library of Congress regional libraries) were combined, there would not be a large selection of books in braille for school-aged readers who are blind. Computerized disks and the publication of larger numbers of literature books in braille for young readers may alleviate this problem. Individualized texts may not be appropriate for children who are blind who are not yet eager to read. Rather, they may be given only as students have "mastered a sizable vocabulary and are independently motivated" (Harley, Truan, & Sanford, 1987, p. 55). There should be some vocabulary control, particularly with regard to words containing braille signs. For children to be successful in reading, teachers must monitor the materials constantly.

Whole Language Approach

Whole language is a "child-centered, literature-based approach to language teaching that immerses students in real communication situations" (Froese, 1991, p. 3). It is a holistic approach to teaching all aspects of language—reading, writing, speaking, and listening—that is dramatically changing the way language and literacy skills are taught. Harp (1991) described it as follows:

> Whole language instruction is a total literacy immersion program. Children read, read, read, and read. They write, write, write and write. They are exposed to whole selections

of literature that confirm what they know about how language works. The focus is first and foremost on the creation of meaning. Only after children understand that reading and writing are meaning creating processes are they exposed to the subskills. And then, [only] as they can benefit from that instruction. (pp. 3-4)

"Whole language is not a practice,...[but] a set of beliefs, a perspective" (Altwerger, Edelsky, & Flores, 1987, p. 145), according to which children are immersed in print-rich environments and empowered to take risks in a variety of meaningful reading and writing activities. Invented spellings and oral reading miscues (errors) are viewed as positive stages in children's emergence as language learners.

Proponents of the whole language approach believe that reading is a meaning-centered process in which meaning progresses from whole language units to their parts. They also believe that reading and writing are parts of an integrated, developmental language process in which children learn to read and write in the same natural way they developed their oral language.

Instructional strategies in this approach include daily SSR reading; daily writing activities, including journal writing; reading predictable trade books; literature-based units of instruction; integrated curricular units; cooperative learning groups; readers' workshops; writers' workshops; and independent and cooperative writing projects. Reutzel and Cooter (1992) noted that many of these strategies may be found in the classrooms of teachers who do not fully subscribe to the whole language approach.

Although the tenets of the whole language approach appear to be sound, there are some unanswered questions. For example, McGee and Richgels (1990) questioned the limited and sometimes contradictory empirical research on whole language. Leu and Kinzer (1991) raised three other concerns as well: (1) Whole language appears to be similar to what has been called good teaching practices in which literacy activities occurred in meaningful contexts; (2) the use of terms like *emergent literacy* and *whole language* may be a problem in that all approaches believe that the acquisition of literacy is emergent or developmental; and (3) it remains a question whether reading and writing should receive equal emphasis in kindergarten programs. Despite these concerns, Leu and Kinzer (1991, p. 140) state that "whole language programs appear to have benefits in motivation and in the amount of writing and reading accomplished by students."

Implications of the Whole Language Approach for Learners Who Are Blind

The child-centered aspect of the whole language approach is a major advantage. The reading program for children who are blind can be tailored to meet their needs and attributes. Because the philosophy of the approach is total literacy immersion, knowledge and skills in reading, writing, and the braille code will be combined in the blind learner's program. The signs and rules of the code will be inferred or will be taught as they are encountered in the reading or writing process.

The whole language approach uses the meaning-centered model of instruction and is a holistic approach. Such an approach permits the learner who reads braille to use his or her skills in the psycholinguistic realm. The use of semantic and syntactical cues will increase the learner's rate of reading and hence comprehension. The child's motivation to read and write is also likely to increase when the emphasis is placed on meaning rather than skills.

If the child who is blind is lacking in language and concept development and in the experiences to provide an adequate schema, he or she may not be ready to read. In reality, as teachers help the child to develop schema, they are employing the whole language approach. Such activities should take precedence over the development of braille code skills or graphophonemic skills because the child is probably not ready for the introduction of such skills. However, as such skills develop, they become part of the schema and knowledge that the child brings to the reading task.

Some would question the use of the whole language approach with the child who is both blind and learning disabled or blind and mentally handicapped. If the skills-centered approach is more effective with children with additional disabilities, the teacher will probably select the interactive model, rather than move totally to a whole language approach. Certainly, research is needed to determine the efficacy of whole language instruction with different populations of children who are blind. After all, an approach that is so child centered should be effective with all children.

Because the whole language approach has been described as a philosophy, rather than as a practice, if the teacher does not subscribe to it, she or he will not apply it. Special teachers may not be familiar with this philosophy or comfortable with it. Although they can obtain information on the approach from books, courses, and workshops, perhaps the best resource for special teachers is the opportunity to work with regular classroom teachers who accept and practice it.

When a blind child is included in a reading program that uses a full or partial whole language approach, the special teacher is a key factor. He or she is responsible for the child's progress in the use of braille writing equipment, including the braillewriter and the slate and stylus, as well as the child's knowledge and use of the braille code. The teacher is also responsible for selecting texts that are appropriate for the child's reading needs and for acquiring them from a somewhat limited supply. Furthermore, it is his or her responsibility to keep the regular teacher alert to the characteristics and needs of the special child whom they are both teaching. Moreover, because this individualized, child-centered program requires more time for preparation and instruction, it seems inconceivable that it could be successful without frequent conferences, visits, and team teaching. And for some learners, particularly in the early stages of literacy, daily contact or even a full-time special teacher is necessary.

In light of these concerns, it is understandable that many teachers can implement only portions of a whole language approach. The important issue is that teachers move toward a meaning-centered approach and that they philosophically accept a holistic view of the development of literacy for children and adults who are blind.

CONTENT AREA READING INSTRUCTION

Content area reading instruction is a philosophy of teaching that spans the K–12 curriculum and involves instruction in each of the subject-matter disciplines. Over 20 years ago, Herber (1970) articulated the content reading philosophy, namely, that functional, meaningful reading instruction involves teaching both *content* (subject matter knowledge) and *process* (appropriate reading strategies) *simultaneously*. He emphasized the need to apply reading strategies directly in the context of instructing students in such subjects as social studies, science, mathematics, home economics, and music and art appreciation, in addition to literature. Herber's views remain consistent with today's need for a knowledge base (content base) in literacy learning.

Aspects of Content Reading

Both Herber (1970) and Early (1964) pointed out basic differences between the processes of "learning to read" and "reading to learn" within the K–12 continuum of instruction that are still relevant today. As Figure 5-5 suggests, as students progress through the K–12 continuum, they receive less and less direct reading instruction (learning to read), but their need to apply reading strategies in content classes to construct meaning increases dramatically (reading to learn).

Indeed, by the time students enter upper-grade-level content classes, many teachers "assume" that they already have developed the necessary skills and strategies to comprehend content reading materials. A major purpose of content reading instruction is to avoid such "assumptive teaching" through the use of a variety of strategies and materials that are designed to teach both content and process at the same time.

If you now refer back to the sample reading passage on "How to Build a New Model Thurboflyer" in Chapter 4, you may gain a clearer understanding of the need for content

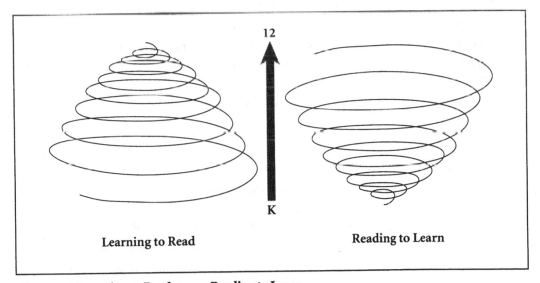

Figure 5-5. Learning to Read versus Reading to Learn

reading instruction. If you were actually assigned this text passage to read independently and then given the 10-item quiz, your teacher would have been guilty of "assumptive teaching." Within the context of this passage, what would your teacher have assumed about you as a reader? Among many assumptions, he or she may have assumed that you

- had adequate knowledge, background, and experience;
- had a strategy or purpose for reading;
- were familiar with the technical terms in the passage;
- could conceptualize the relationships among the technical terms;
- had an interest in the topic;
- were motivated to read the passage;
- could visualize a Thurboflyer;
- could follow the directions and actually build a Thurboflyer;
- could follow the structure of the text;
- could relate the relevance of Thurboflyers to your personal learning;
- could retain the basic text information.

Or, your teacher simply may have assumed that you should have "learned to read" in elementary school and that, at any rate, his or her job is not to teach reading, but to teach the content of Thurboflyers. This is assumptive teaching!

In the late 1960s and early 1970s, Herber and his associates developed a number of strategies for reading secondary school content that were related to content vocabulary, textbook structures, concept development, levels of comprehension, questioning strategies, readers' attitudes, small-group interactions, and so forth. These strategies were designed, in part, to avoid the practice of assumptive teaching, and most of them have been adapted for use in the elementary grades.

Over the past 20 years, numerous content-reading strategies and materials have been reported in the literature. There are far too many of them to mention by name, but they do share several characteristics. In general, they each tend to

- be consistent with the constructive, interactive, and strategic reading process,
- emphasize a more integrated language approach, particularly in the area of reading-writing relationships,
- teach subject matter content and process at the same time,
- use content reading materials as the vehicles of instruction,
- empower content teachers as those who are the most qualified to teach content reading,
- empower students as active participants in learning,
- use variations of cooperative learning during instruction.

Implications of Content Reading for Learners Who Are Blind

As with children with normal vision, much instructional time during the first two or three years of school is devoted to reading. The importance attached to learning to read is demonstrated by the way services are provided to the child who is blind. During this period, the itinerant special education teacher makes several visits per week or perhaps daily and plays a teaching role, rather than a consultative role.

During the learning-to-read stage, the teacher concentrates on helping the child to develop adequate schema. Language and concept development are part of the child's curriculum. Field trips, real and simulated experiences, and reading to the child are strategies to develop the schema for the narrative reading that takes place during this stage. Stories tend to be about events and people who are familiar to the child who is blind. Both the regular and special teacher help the child learn to read for meaning and to develop skills that become part of the child's knowledge for meaningful reading. The special teacher uses this time to incorporate instruction related to the braille code, its signs and rules, into the materials that the blind child reads, so that by the end of third grade, the child has been introduced to most of the contractions, short forms, and other special signs.

And so, by the time the child enters the reading-to-learn stage, the special educator also becomes an assumptive teacher. That is, the teacher assumes that the child has learned to read and that weekly or fewer visits are adequate. The child is integrated to an increasing extent into the social and physical sciences, health, and mathematics—the content reading areas. The reading text is no longer narrative; it is expository and content specific. The reader who is blind may lack knowledge because of limited experiences, limited concept development, and limited reading experiences at a time when reading instruction has decreased or even been terminated.

It is at this reading-to-learn stage that students who are blind tend to make heavy use of recorded materials and human personal readers—and well they should, if they are taught to use these resources properly. It would be regrettable, however, if the use of auditory reading decreases the students' reading instruction and opportunities to further their literacy skills of reading and writing. Therefore, it is important to maintain a balance between braille and recorded materials.

Strategies used by the regular classroom teacher—such as directed reading activity, study guides, marginal notes, and even semantic mapping—will be effective with the child who is blind. The special teacher should also use strategies to increase the student's reading proficiency by monitoring his or her knowledge and use of the braille code. Writing tasks increase during this reading-to-learn stage, and a parallel "writing-to-learn" stage emerges when content reading increases. Instruction leads to literacy, and literacy in either area—reading or writing—enhances the development of literacy in the other.

INSTRUCTIONAL FRAMEWORKS

Leu and Kinzer (1991) described three instructional frameworks (see Figure 5-6) that focus on the classroom teacher and classroom teaching rather than on the type of instructional approach (i.e., basal reader, language experience, etc.) as described earlier in the chapter. According to Leu and Kinzer, a classroom teacher's instruction can be described as following (1) a *materials framework*, based on a published set of materials and lesson-planning infor-

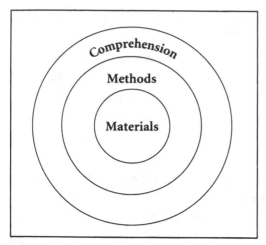

Figure 5-6. Instructional Frameworks. Source: Based on *Effective Reading Instruction, K-8*, 2nd ed., by D. J. Leu and C. K. Kinzer, 1991, New York: Merrill.

mation; (2) a *methods framework*, based on certain procedural steps contained in one or more instructional methods; or (3) a *comprehension framework*, based on personal beliefs about the components of reading, how people read, and how reading is taught. "A comprehension framework," according to Leu and Kinzer (p. 15), "is the most powerful and flexible of the three frameworks [and] is what most effective teachers strive for."

It makes sense to evaluate the teaching of reading from the classroom teacher's point of view and how she or he implements instruction in the classroom. Conversely, it makes little sense to evaluate the teaching of reading on the basis of "surface labels," such as "phonics," "sight word," "basal readers," linguistic," "holistic instruction," "whole language," and "language experience," without knowing the specific teaching strategies used in the classroom. Leu and Kinzer's three instructional frameworks provide a basis for describing and evaluating classroom-based reading instruction.

Materials Framework

Within the context of Leu and Kinzer's conceptualization of instructional frameworks, teachers who teach reading within a materials framework basically organize their teaching around the set of published materials with which they are provided. Furthermore, they organize their daily lessons around teachers' manuals that specify stories to read, objectives to meet, activities to pursue, skills to teach, workbook pages to complete, and, ultimately, tests to administer. Typically, lesson plans in many teachers' manuals follow the directed reading activity (DRA) format that was discussed under the basal reader approach.

Teachers who teach within materials frameworks basically follow commercially published programs and guidelines, whether their programs involve phonics instruction, linguistics instruction, basal reader stories, literature-based instruction, or even published programs that assert that they are "whole language" programs.

Methods Framework

Teachers who teach reading within a methods framework organize their teaching around the use of a variety of instructional methods or strategies involving certain procedural steps or structures. These methods, or strategies, can be adapted to the variety of narrative and expository readings that students complete. Methods frameworks are potentially empowering, since they allow teachers to go beyond the restrictions of published lesson plans and adapt the most appropriate methods and strategies for their own classrooms.

A few examples of methods-framework strategies and the accompanying procedural steps include these:

- *DRTA: directed reading thinking activities*—predicting text outcomes, actively reading, and confirming or denying predictions of the text.
- *SQ3R: surveying text, questioning text, reading text, reciting answers to questions, and reviewing text.*
- *Process writing:* Prewriting, drafting, revising, editing, and publishing.
- *Individualized reading:* self-selecting text readings, independently reading text, having conferences with teachers, and completing projects related to text applications.
- *Language experience activities:* Identifying meaningful real-life experiences, eliciting oral language descriptions, transcribing oral language to written language, helping children read written descriptions.
- *K-W-L:* Identifying what students already *know* about key concepts before they read text, identifying what they *want* to learn from the reading, and identifying what new information they *learned* from the reading.
- *Cooperative learning groups:* Identifying group goals, assigning students to groups (normally heterogeneous), completing group goals, and sharing group conclusions.

There are numerous other methods or strategies for teaching reading that do not involve specified procedural steps. In general, teachers who are familiar with a wide range of reading strategies are better able to adapt their instruction to the needs of their classrooms than are teachers who follow a step-by-step approach to teaching reading that is dictated by prescriptive teaching materials.

Comprehension Framework

Teachers who teach reading within a comprehension framework organize their teaching on the basis of the knowledge and beliefs related to components of reading (see Chapter 4), how one reads, and how reading ability develops. Figure 5-7 presents a continuum of beliefs related to the question, How does one read? (Leu & Kinzer, 1991). At the left end of the continuum are those who believe that reading is a text-based process in which readers initially decode text print into words, sentences, and paragraphs to determine the literal, or explicit, meaning of the text. This text-based processing is analogous to a skills-centered approach to reading. At the right extreme of the continuum are those who believe that reading is a reader-based process in which readers use knowledge from their experiential background to predict meaning from text. This reader-based processing is analogous to a meaning-centered approach to reading. An interactive point of view, represented in the middle of the continuum, suggests that constructing meaning involves combining text-based information with reader-based predictions that are based on the reader's schema. Where do your present beliefs fall on this continuum?

Figure 5-8 represents a continuum of beliefs related to the question, How does reading ability develop? (Leu & Kinzer, 1991). At the left end of the continuum are those who believe that reading ability develops through the direct, deductive teaching of specific reading skills related to decoding, vocabulary development, and comprehension. At the right end of the continuum are those who believe

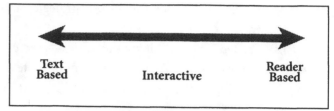

Figure 5-7. How Does One Read? Source: Based on *Effective Reading Instruction, K-8*, 2nd ed., by D. J. Leu and C. K. Kinzer, 1991, New York: Merrill.

that reading ability develops through holistic language instruction that provides print-rich and language-rich environments in which students develop functional reading and writing abilities inductively. The integrated point of view, represented in the middle of the continuum, suggests that the development of skills is necessary, at times, within the context of comprehending larger language units. Where do your beliefs fall on this continuum?

Your responses to the questions asked with regard to Figures 5-7 and 5-8 provide some perspective on your beliefs about reading instruction. Figure 5-9 contrasts the characteristics of one skills-centered approach—basal reader instruction—and a meaning-centered approach—whole language instruction. As you read the items in the figure, keep in mind that individual teachers who hold to either approach

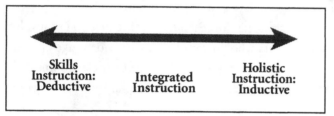

Figure 5-8. How Does Reading Ability Develop? Source: Based on *Effective Reading Instruction, K-8*, 2nd ed., by D. J. Leu and C. K. Kinzer, 1991, New York: Merrill.

could teach within a *materials* framework, a *methods* framework, or a *comprehension* framework.

Implications of Three Instructional Frameworks for Teaching Reading to Learners Who Are Blind

The three instructional frameworks presented focus on the teacher and on teaching, not on the models, approaches, or strategies that were previously presented. Leu and Kinzer (1991) have the regular classroom in mind when they present their views. Students who are blind learn to read in a variety of "classrooms"—residential schools, resource rooms, an itinerant teacher's work area, with a teacher-consultant somewhere in the classroom environs, or in a classroom with their sighted peers.

When the reader is blind, the teachers who function within one of these frameworks are known as regular education teachers or as special education teachers. The special teachers are usually further classified by the program (classroom) in which they work. The special teacher has had specialized preparation to teach children who are blind and who read

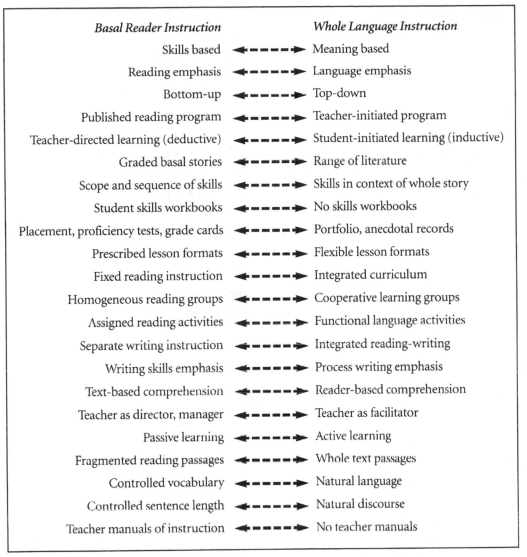

Basal Reader Instruction		Whole Language Instruction
Skills based	◄− − − − ►	Meaning based
Reading emphasis	◄− − − − ►	Language emphasis
Bottom-up	◄− − − − ►	Top-down
Published reading program	◄− − − − ►	Teacher-initiated program
Teacher-directed learning (deductive)	◄− − − − ►	Student-initiated learning (inductive)
Graded basal stories	◄− − − − ►	Range of literature
Scope and sequence of skills	◄− − − − ►	Skills in context of whole story
Student skills workbooks	◄− − − − ►	No skills workbooks
Placement, proficiency tests, grade cards	◄− − − − ►	Portfolio, anecdotal records
Prescribed lesson formats	◄− − − − ►	Flexible lesson formats
Fixed reading instruction	◄− − − − ►	Integrated curriculum
Homogeneous reading groups	◄− − − − ►	Cooperative learning groups
Assigned reading activities	◄− − − − ►	Functional language activities
Separate writing instruction	◄− − − − ►	Integrated reading-writing
Writing skills emphasis	◄− − − − ►	Process writing emphasis
Text-based comprehension	◄− − − − ►	Reader-based comprehension
Teacher as director, manager	◄− − − − ►	Teacher as facilitator
Passive learning	◄− − − − ►	Active learning
Fragmented reading passages	◄− − − − ►	Whole text passages
Controlled vocabulary	◄− − − − ►	Natural language
Controlled sentence length	◄− − − − ►	Natural discourse
Teacher manuals of instruction	◄− − − − ►	No teacher manuals

Figure 5-9. Characteristics of Basal Reader and Whole Language Instruction

braille. It is unusual for regular teachers to have had this special preparation, but it is likely that they will have had some preparation in the teaching of reading.

The blind child may be taught to read by a regular classroom teacher, by a special reading teacher, by a special education teacher, or by a team of teachers. As regular classrooms include more and more students who are blind, many will be taught in classroom-based programs, and many will be taught by a team of teachers. As we focus on the teacher functioning within one of the frameworks, we prefer not to identify a particular category of teachers. While the implications may vary somewhat from one group of teachers to another, the consideration of instructional frameworks has similar application for the teacher, regardless of the role he or she assumes.

Materials Framework

The teacher of blind children who adopts the materials framework uses a set of published materials, such as the basal reader series or whole language materials. Whatever their beliefs, there is likely to be a set of materials to guide teachers in providing reading instruction. If the regular teacher and special teacher function as a team, they should also select the materials as a team.

Teachers choose to work in the materials framework for a number of reasons. First, the school system may choose it and select the materials to be used. Second, new teachers may choose the framework during their first year of teaching until they gain confidence and competence. (The certified teacher of the blind who has minimal preparation in teaching reading may choose this framework for the same reason.) Although it may seem paradoxical, the materials framework may be chosen because of the lack of materials in braille; that is, the teacher tends to move into this framework because only basal readers—either the special braille series *Patterns* or transliterated copies—are accessible. As other materials (texts) become available in braille, teachers of students who are blind will probably use prepared sets less frequently or in a less structured fashion.

Methods Framework

In the methods framework, the teacher makes more choices—in the materials to be used and the strategies for instruction. Strategies may include any of those mentioned earlier, as well as others, some of which the teacher will devise. The child who is blind can benefit from almost any of these strategies, which may be implemented in any program structure, from full-time mainstreaming to a full-time residential program. The strategies may be implemented by the special educator, the regular teacher, or the team. They may use basal reader materials, though not in the prescriptive presentation found in the teacher's guide, or most other materials related to the various methods or strategies, from the text-based process to the interactive process to the reader-based process. The teacher's beliefs about reading provide the guidelines.

Comprehension Framework

In the comprehension framework, teachers are required to make decisions about a broad range of materials and methods and how to use them. The framework goes beyond the knowledge required to make such choices. It stipulates that teachers make clear decisions about how they believe reading takes place and develops.

On the basis of their beliefs, both regular classroom teachers and special educators will use the comprehension framework to choose materials and methods or adapt methods or materials that respond to how the child who is blind reads or how his or her reading ability develops (Leu & Kinzer, 1991). Thus, teachers who use portions of *Patterns*, language experience stories, and cooperative learning or other strategies and decide how to meld these materials and methods for the greatest benefit of their learners who are blind have adopted a comprehension framework of reading instruction. For the special or regular educator who teaches a child who is blind to read, the comprehension framework offers more flexibility in instructional decision making than do the other frameworks. The comprehension framework allows the teacher to choose what seems best for each individual learner and to make changes when the choice is not effective in helping the child progress toward constructive, interactive reading.

The decision as to which framework the teacher of children who read braille will choose will be relatively easy if he or she works alone as a regular or special teacher. The choice may change as a teacher grows professionally. Choices are more difficult when more than one person is involved. Need for teachers who work as a team to make team decisions was mentioned earlier. Each teacher makes contributions to the decision, each carrying more weight at different times. Sometimes the regular classroom teacher will predominate, directed by the very nature of the classroom or the school system. Sometimes it is the special teacher, directed by the needs of the blind child or by the availability or lack of braille materials. Members of the team can help one another to choose an individual framework and to grow within that framework. While the instructional framework focuses on the teachers, the teachers must focus on their student who is blind and reads braille.

SUMMARY

Perhaps the two most meaningful observations in this chapter are that there is no best method for teaching reading and that the classroom teacher is the most important variable in determining effective reading instruction. These statements should become the guidelines—even the principles—for teachers of children who are blind, in considering models, approaches, and strategies for teaching reading.

This chapter reviewed a number of different models of reading instruction—the meaning-centered, skills-centered, and interactive models—from which teachers can select, depending on the needs and competencies of the child who is blind. Different schools and teachers will apply these models through one or more specific approaches to teaching reading, including the basal reader, language experience, literature based, and whole language. Examining instructional frameworks that focus on the classroom teacher and teaching provides a different way to evaluate reading instruction.

The teacher is the key to blind students' learning to read and reading to learn. Since there is no one best method, the teacher is free to make instructional decisions. The students' individual differences and needs should be the most important consideration in making these decisions, and the teacher's own beliefs about reading will be the guide.

REFERENCES

Altwerger, B., Edelsky, C., & Flores, B. M. (1987). Whole language: What's new? *The Reading Teacher, 41*(2), 144-154.

Anderson, R. C., Hiebert, E. H., Scott, J. A., & Wilkinson, I. A. G. (1985). *Becoming a nation of readers: The report of the Commission on Reading.* Washington, DC: National Academy of Education, National Institute of Education.

Bleiberg, R. (1970). Is there a need for specially designed reading series for beginning blind readers? *The New Outlook for the Blind, 64,* 135-138.

Bond, G. L., & Dykstra, R. (1967). The cooperative research program in first grade reading instruction. *Reading Research Quarterly,* 5-142.

Carbo, M., Dunn, R., & Dunn, K. (1986). *Teaching students to read through their individual learning styles.* Reston, VA: Prentice-Hall.

Caton, H. (1979). A primary reading program for beginning braille readers. *Journal of Visual Impairment & Blindness, 73*(8), 309-313.

Caton, H., & Bradley, E. J. (1978-79, Fall). A new approach to beginning braille reading. *Education of the Visually Handicapped,* 66-71.

Caton, H. R, Pester, E., & Bradley, E. J. (1980) *Patterns: The primary braille reading program.* Louisville, KY: American Printing House for the Blind.

Early, M. (1964). The meaning of reading instruction in secondary schools. *Journal of Reading, 8,* 25-29.

Flood, J., & Lapp, O. (1986). Types of texts: The match between what students read in basals and what they encounter in tests. *Reading Research Quarterly, 21,* 284-297.

Froese, V. (1991). Introduction to whole language teaching and learning. In V. Froese (Ed.), *Whole language: Practice and theory* (pp. 1-16). Boston: Allyn & Bacon.

Goodman, K. (1976). Reading: A psycholinguistic guessing game. In H. Singer & R. Ruddell (Eds.), *Theoretical models and processes of reading* (2nd ed.). Newark, DE: International Reading Association.

Harley, R. K., Truan, M. B., & Sanford, L. D. (1987). *Communication skills for visually impaired learners.* Springfield, IL: Charles C Thomas.

Harp, B. (1991). Principles of assessment and evaluation in whole language classrooms. In B. Harp (Ed.), *Assessment and evaluation in whole language programs* (pp. 35-50). Norwood, MA: Christopher-Gordon.

Herber, H. L. (1970). *Teaching reading in content areas.* Englewood Cliffs, NJ: Prentice-Hall.

Leu, D. J., & Kinzer, C. K. (1991). *Effective reading instruction K-8* (2nd ed.). New York: Merrill.

Lowenfeld, B., Abel, G. L., & Hattlen, P. H. (1969). *Blind children learn to read.* Springfield, IL: Charles C Thomas.

Mason, J. M., & Au, K. H. (1990). *Reading instruction for today.* Glenview, IL: Scott, Foresman.

McGee, L. M., & Richgels, O. J. (1990). *Literacy beginnings: Supporting young readers and writers.* Boston: Allyn & Bacon.

Reutzel, D. R., & Cooter, R. B. (1992). *Teaching children To read: From basals to books.* New York: Merrill.

Rex, E. J. (1970). An analysis of braille features in basal readers. *Education for the Visually Handicapped, 2*(4), 97-107.

Rex, E. J. (1971). Experimental instructional materials for teaching reading in braille. *Education for the Visually Handicapped, 3*(1), 1-6.

Vacca, J. L., Vacca, R. T., & Gove, M. K. (1991). *Reading and learning to read* (2nd ed.). Boston: Little, Brown.

Weaver, C. (1994). *Reading process and practice* (rev. ed.). Portsmouth, NH: Heinemann.

BRAILLE WRITING LITERACY: APPROACHES AND STRATEGIES

A revolution is taking place in the way writing is taught in schools throughout the country. In the traditional skills-centered approach to writing instruction, students generally complete artificial, often fragmented writing tasks and then receive feedback on errors and grades on their papers. This focus on the outcome of writing—the written product—is rapidly being balanced or replaced by the meaning-centered approach, which concentrates on the process a writer goes through to arrive at a final product. The meaning-centered approach ensures that the purpose for writing is clear and useful and that the writing holds value for the student. These contrasting views of writing are shown in the two scenarios on the next page.

In the current wave of excitement sweeping the country about new approaches to writing, there are more and more classrooms like Ms. Woolery's in the second scenario. Traditional skills-centered classrooms, where students often dread writing and feel it has little purpose, are rapidly being replaced by meaning-centered classrooms, where students are excited about writing and see its purpose and value in their lives.

Students who are blind receive writing instruction in both types of classrooms. The role of the teacher of students with visual impairments varies greatly, depending on the instructional arrangement. However, regardless of the educational setting and the approach to writing instruction, the special teacher will not only provide instruction in the unique aspects of writing in braille in the context of meaningful writing tasks, but will also expand the student's repertoire of writing tools to allow direct communication with persons with normal vision through regular print.

To help you understand how different approaches to writing instruction influence the teaching of writing to students who are blind, this chapter discusses two global approaches or models: skills-centered and meaning-centered instruction. (Although the concepts of skills-centered and meaning-centered instruction have been applied to overall models of, as

SCENARIO 1: A SKILLS-CENTERED CLASSROOM

At Mason Elementary School, Sarah, a second grader, is nervously waiting for her teacher to return the story she wrote yesterday. She has a low C in writing this semester and is hoping for an A or B on this paper to bring up her average.

Mr. Clements asked everyone in the third grade to write a story about what had happened during the Thanksgiving holiday. Sarah wrote about the family trip to her grandparents' farm in rural Kentucky. She wrote about helping her Grandma gather eggs from the henhouse, riding on her Grandpa's tractor, and feeding the pigs. To show that there were a lot of flies in the pig pen, she dotted the "i" in "pigs" with a picture of a bug!

The first thing Sarah sees when Mr. Clements hands back her story is a big red C and the words, "needs work." Mr. Clements noted corrections for five spelling errors, three punctuation errors, and an "awk." (Sarah wondered what an "awk" was—it sounded terrible!) There were two other notes on her paper. The first said, "Let's work on our penmanship." And the other, written next to the picture of the bug, said "Please use a dot."

Sarah slumps in her chair and sighs. She thinks to herself, "I thought this was a *great* story, and I was just sure it would get at least a B. Next time I'll try really hard to get all the words spelled right and see if I can do better with those punctuation marks. But what will I do about that 'awk'? Really, I wish we could just do more math instead of writing!"

SCENARIO 2: A MEANING-CENTERED CLASSROOM

At Franklin Elementary School, Matthew and a lot of other students are writing in their personal journals. Matthew loves this part of the day! He is writing about his weekend trip to the museum, where he saw a huge dinosaur. Matthew draws a picture of a dinosaur at the top of the page and a few boulders in the margins. He titles his journal entry "I Saw a Dinasore" and starts writing.

The classroom buzzes with activity. Ms. Woolery is moving from desk to desk as her students are busy writing. She helps Carlos explore ideas for making a birthday card for his mother. Marcie appears troubled by an article she is writing for the school paper, so Ms. Woolery listens to her concerns and helps her consider other perspectives on the story. As she comes to Matthew, he shows her his journal. Ms. Woolery reads with great interest and comments, "I have seen that dinosaur—it *is* huge! What else happened?"

Kate, Celeste, and Mario are in the Publishing Center making covers for books that are being "published" by the third-grade class. Yesterday, they worked with other students to do the final editing on these books. Ms. Woolery was a big help and taught them how to use three dots together to show that part of a sentence was missing. It was neat! (But what was that thing called?)

In social studies, all the students are beginning to write reports on their family histories for a class anthology. Today they are just thinking about what they might write and how. Some students are drawing pictures of their families, while others are sketching out their family trees. Everyone knows they will have a wonderful Christmas present for their parents this year!

well as approaches to, teaching reading literacy, in discussions of writing they are often considered specific instructional approaches.) This chapter also presents the role of microcomputers in facilitating writing instruction, along with implications for students who are blind, and includes suggestions for teaching the unique skills of writing to students who are blind.

APPROACHES TO WRITING INSTRUCTION

As Chapter 5 did for reading instruction, this chapter discusses the skills-centered and meaning-centered approaches to writing instruction. It should be noted, however, that in actual practice teachers often use elements of both. Such an approach, regardless of whether it concentrates more on meaning or on skills, is referred to as "interactive."

Skills-Centered Approach

Components of Writing

The traditional skills-centered approach to teaching writing generally segments various components of writing into three areas—spelling, English, and penmanship—and provides a separate textbook for each area to teach specific skills and subskills. In the spelling program, students learn 10 to 20 new words each week throughout the elementary grades. In the English program, they learn a variety of skills such as grammar, usage, conventions, and various forms of writing (for example, friendly and business letters). In the area of penmanship, students first learn to hold a pencil, position the paper, and form acceptable manuscript letters and then learn to form the cursive counterparts. Such an approach presumes that students will integrate the various subskills and generalize them to real writing.

Noyce and Christie (1989) used the term *compartmentalization* to refer to the separation of the various parts of the language arts curriculum[1] and stated that "rarely are the different aspects of written language linked together in any meaningful way" (p. 2). Another typical problem with the traditional approach is *fragmentation*, in which instruction "focuses on discrete subskills that are divorced from real texts or meaningful situations" (Noyce & Christie, p. 2). Unfortunately, the compartmentalization and fragmentation of the language arts curriculum often result in lack of transfer between the various components. For example, correct spelling of words learned in spelling class may not transfer to writing a story in English class. A growing body of research has cast "doubt on the soundness of traditional, compartmentalized approaches to language and arts instruction" (Noyce & Christie, p. 3).

Degree of Emphasis on Writing

Graves (1984) conducted two studies of the amount of emphasis placed on writing in commonly used language arts textbooks. The first study, conducted in 1976, revealed that when writing was addressed, textbooks focused primarily on grammar and punctuation and paid

---

[1]These authors refer to all aspects of the language arts curriculum, including reading. Since this chapter focuses on writing, the discussion here will concentrate on typical components of language arts that relate to writing—spelling, English, and penmanship. It should be noted, however, that to be truly meaningful to students, writing should always be linked to and integrated with reading.

little attention to composition. This research led Graves to conclude that "most writing instruction really isn't instruction at all. Rather, the teacher provides the appointment for writing through assignments and then responds to mechanical errors contained in the child's writing after it is completed. The entire process area is left untouched by the texts" (p. 59).

In his 1983 study, Graves (1984) found that since 1976, there had been no major changes in the way writing was taught through language arts textbooks or in the level of emphasis devoted to writing. For example, he found that a second-grade text devoted only 6 out of 209 pages to the process of writing and that a fifth-grade text devoted only 9 out of 407 pages to it. In some cases, Graves found less attention to writing in 1983 than in 1976. As a strong proponent of a process-centered approach to writing, Graves concluded that language arts textbooks were of little value in teaching writing when he wrote:

> The few attempts to teach writing can only be described as horrendous. Books are still filled with story and picture starters. Topics are almost always given to children, thereby suggesting that children are without topics of their own. Writers should write about what they know. How can textbooks presume to know what individual children know? [p. 53]

DeGroff and Leu (1987) found similar sobering results in another study of language arts textbooks.

Focus on Product

In the traditional skills-centered approach, the product—the final outcome of a writing activity—is the focus of attention. This approach tends to be teacher centered, since the teacher is the primary audience for writing activities and the primary responder (Harp, 1991). Generally, writing experiences are fabricated for the purposes of teaching a specific skill or set of skills and, therefore, have no real purpose or personal value to the student; hence, the student feels no ownership of the writing he or she has completed.

For example, students who are learning to write business letters may be asked to write the Acme Pencil Company and request a refund on a box of 100 pencils with no erasers. Such an activity has no real meaning to students, since they have no such eraserless pencils in hand and thus see no reason to write such letters. This activity, then, is purely teacher centered because the teacher assigned the activity and will ultimately grade it. Furthermore, the activity is likely to yield one linear draft (Harp, 1991) of the letter without the chance to revise or edit it before "sending" it.

Another Perspective

With the new wave of reform in writing instruction, it is difficult these days to find advocates of the strict skills-centered approach to teaching writing. This does not mean, however, that language arts textbooks completely lack merit. As with any subject, it is the teacher who makes instruction meaningful and useful to children—not the textbook. Textbooks can be a valuable resource for the skillful teacher who uses only those parts that will achieve a real purpose in the classroom. It is the teacher who is responsible for making appropriate linkages between various parts of the language arts curriculum. The practice of "writing across the curriculum" is one example of the way to integrate writing with other skills and to ensure that it generalizes throughout a student's life. The skills-centered approach to teaching writing is not necessarily incompatible with the meaning-centered approach. When elements of both are used, the approach is considered "interactive."

Meaning-Centered Approach

Purposefulness

At the heart of the meaning-centered approach to writing is purpose: "Students must see a purpose for writing. They must feel that they have something to say about the topic. Students should not be asked to write unless the purpose is clear to them and genuine use is to be made of the writing" (Sampson, Van Allen, & Sampson, 1991). The meaning-centered approach to writing establishes and fosters an environment for writing in which there is a clear connection between writing experiences and the role they play in communication in real life. Farnan, Lapp, and Flood (1992, p. 555) wrote that "real writing has real consequences. It is purposeful, with content and context which are meaningful to the writer." Some real purposes of writing are presented in Table 6-1.

Table 6-1. Real Purposes of Writing

Books	Poems	Lists (for shopping, gifts,
Stories	Diaries	parties, trips, things to do)
Reviews (of books, movies,	Scripts/plays	Calendars
restaurants, products)	Comic strips	Messages
Author page (for books)	Rules	Bulletins
Directions	Proposals	Posters
Notices	Invitations	Signs
Newspaper articles	Journals	Charts
Reports	Crossword puzzles	Letters
Interviews	Dedications	Postcards
How-to manuals	Brochures	Conversations
Advice columns	Newsletters	Want ads
Surveys	Anthologies	Announcements
Questionnaires	Yearbooks	Song lyrics
Evaluations	Book blurbs	Magazine articles
Instructions	Thank you letters	Guides
Essays	Greeting cards	Assignments
Advertisements	Summaries	Commercials
Memos	Recipes	

Source: *Invitations: Changing as Teachers and Learners K-12* (p. 171), by R. Routman, 1991, Portsmouth, NH: Heinemann. Copyright © 1991, Heinemann, a division of Reed Publishing (USA), Inc. Reprinted by permission of Regie Routman.

Table 6-2. Guidelines for Teaching Functional Writing

Principle 1: Purpose governs all classroom writing

A. Every writing experience should begin with the identification of a purpose and an audience.

B. Purposes should emerge from classroom activities and interests but, if at times they come from an outside source, children should agree that they are worth writing for.

C. Once a purpose is identified, children and teacher should select the appropriate forms, styles, conventions, and mechanics for meeting it, adapting what they already know to the need and learning whatever new elements are necessary.

D. Instruction in spelling, usage, punctuation, and capitalization should be integrated into writing, not taught in isolation. If an item does not come up naturally in writing, perhaps it is not necessary for children of this age to learn it.

E. Since workbooks, worksheets, and drill exercises are not related to any purposes of real world writing, they should not be used in the classroom.

F. Completed written work should be judged by its effectiveness in serving its purpose and reaching its audience.

Principle 2: Children do real-world writing

A. The distinction between public and private writing and their attendant characteristics should be made. Public writing goes to a large and/or unfamiliar audience who will judge it at least partly on neatness and correctness; private writing is for one's self or one's intimates and is judged on communicative effectiveness alone.

B. Classroom writing tasks should reflect—although they cannot duplicate—the range of writing tasks that people do in the real world, from lists, to messages, to poetry.

C. Before writing, children need a time for thinking, planning, and oral exploration of a topic.

D. The writing process should cover sufficient time—preferably a period of several days—so that children can talk about, think about, revise, and recopy their work before calling it done.

The purposefulness and functionality of writing go hand in hand. When children write with a focused purpose, their writing fulfills a functional need in communicating a message to an intended audience. A meaning-centered approach to teaching writing is based on the belief that writing must have a purpose and, therefore, must be functional in one's daily life. To address the need for a functional approach to teaching writing, Yatvin (1981) outlined the elements of such a program for middle school students (although the same ideas and concepts apply to learners of all ages). She defined a functional approach as "one that adopts the motivations and methods of people writing in the real world" (p. 43) and presented three basic principles of functionalism:[2]

    1. Purpose governs all classroom writing. Not only do students have a real purpose for everything they write, but all formal, technical, and stylistic considerations grow out of that purpose.

---

[2]These principles outlined Yatvin's "wish list" for a functional writing program and, therefore, were written in a future tense ("Purpose *would* govern..."). Since they represent the essence of a meaning-centered approach today, all verbs have been changed to the present tense. Otherwise, the principles are quoted verbatim.

Table 6-2. *(Continued)*

E. Finished written work that is going to a public audience should be neat and correct, just as effective examples of public writing in the real world are.

F. Children should not be asked to tinker with prepared writing samples deliberately loaded with errors and confusing choices. Such exercises are not a part of real world writing.

G. Teachers should not write comments, corrections, or grades on completed papers for which they are not the audience. They may comment orally or on a separate sheet of paper, remembering that the time for improving this piece of writing is past.

Principle 3: Teaching is a supportive process

A. Classroom writing should be a group effort in which teachers and other students act as collaborators, editors, and critics all along the way.

B. Instruction before writing should include models or frames, oral exploration of the topic, demonstration of proper use of mechanics likely to be needed, and the development of a plan for writing. The object of preparation is to make children feel they can handle the task.

C. At every step of the writing process, children should have full access to the people and materials that can help them, whether their needs are for information, words, spelling, or reactions to what they've written so far.

D. All pieces of public writing need a thorough editing phase which includes emotional reactions, substantive criticism, and technical assistance.

E. Since more than sixty years of educational research have failed to demonstrate that a knowledge of formal grammar helps people to write better, grammar instruction should not be a part of writing instruction.

Source: "A Functional Writing Program for the Middle Grades" (pp. 43-57), by J. Yatvin, 1981, in S. Haley-James (Ed.), *Perspectives on Writing in Grades 1-8*, Urbana, IL: National Council of Teachers of English. Copyright © 1981, National Council of Teachers of English. Excerpted by permission.

2. As far as possible, children do the various kinds of writing people do in the real world and follow the same kinds of procedures.

3. Teaching is a supportive process. Rather than concentrating efforts on instruction separate from writing or post-writing correction, teachers provide assistance throughout the writing process (p. 44).

Guidelines for implementing these principles (Yatvin, 1981) are presented in Table 6-2.

Several "themes" that emerge from these guidelines are characteristic of the meaning-centered approach to teaching writing. First, to make any writing meaningful, one initiates the writing task by identifying its purpose and the audience that it is intended to affect. Second, the process of writing receives primary emphasis in all writing activities. The written product, although important, is judged by how effective it is in achieving its intended purpose; this is called rhetorical effectiveness. Third, the teaching of written language conventions (such as spelling and punctuation) should emerge from the needs identified as students engage in real writing tasks. Advocates of the meaning-centered approach (see, for example, Atwell, 1987; Calkins, 1986; Graves, 1983, 1984; Routman, 1988, 1991; Yatvin, 1981) are strongly opposed to the use of worksheets, fill-in-the-blank exercises, and other fabricated activities to teach writing. Finally, the role of the teacher is to support students while they engage in the writing process, not simply to give assignments and grade the resulting products.

Process

As reflected in Yatvin's (1981) guidelines, a meaning-centered approach emphasizes the process of writing, rather than only the product. Leu and Kinzer (1991, p. 364) defined process writing as "a view of writing instruction that supports each of the elements of the writing process: prewriting, drafting, revising, editing, and publishing." Harp (1991) summarized some significant differences between process-centered and product-centered writing (see Table 6-3).

It is important to remember that process writing, as a feature of meaning-centered writing instruction, is meaningful to students only when the writing activity has a real purpose in their lives. Not all process writing is necessarily meaningful or purposeful to students. As in the example of the business letter to Acme Pencil Company, the teacher may indeed use a process approach to completing this activity by facilitating students through the various elements of the writing process. However, since the original task was fabricated (in that no eraserless pencils existed and, hence, there was no reason to write a letter requesting a refund), the writing experience lacks purpose and meaning. In the meaning-centered approach to writing, the teacher ensures that the task is meaningful and purposeful at the outset and then supports the various elements of the writing process throughout the experience.

Supporting the writing process is much more than teaching students a sequential series of steps to follow, from prewriting to publishing. Routman (1991, p. 164) stated that this kind of application, "doing writing process," is not valid. Rather, the meaning-centered classroom embraces the writing process holistically and integrates it into all writing activities.

Table 6-3. A Comparison of Process and Product Writing

When We Write as a Process	When We Write for a Product
The writing is student centered.	The writing is teacher centered.
The teacher's role is to model and coach.	The teacher's role is to assign and grade.
We write for many audiences.	The teacher is the primary audience.
The process is evaluated.	The product is graded.
The editing group or editing committee is the primary responder.	The teacher is the primary responder.
We write many, ever-improving drafts.	We write one linear draft.
The entire process of thinking, writing, revising, editing, and publishing is done in class.	A draft is done in class.

Source: "Principles of Assessment and Evaluation in Whole Language Classrooms" (p. 43), by B. Harp, 1991, in B. Harp (Ed.) *Assessment and Evaluation in Whole Language Programs,* Norwood, MA: Christopher-Gordon. Copyright © 1991, Christopher-Gordon Publishers, Inc. Reprinted by permission.

Whole Language

The whole language approach, which was discussed in Chapter 5, fully supports the process approach to writing and the need for writing to have purpose and meaning in children's lives. However, it is erroneous to equate whole language with a meaning-centered approach to teaching writing, since whole language is much more. In whole language instruction, there is no distinction between reading and writing as separate parts of the total language curriculum. Nevertheless, this chapter concentrates on those aspects of the approach that are related to writing.

As part of the belief that "language is a naturally developing human activity," whole language recognizes children's earliest attempts at writing—generally drawing and scribbling—as meaning being composed on paper. Leu and Kinzer (1991) stated that "the concept of emergent literacy . . . implies that students' written products are communicative acts in a state of evolution, thus students' written work should be considered meaningful and should be encouraged, shared, and highlighted" (p. 138). As children emerge as writers, they typically use five forms: scribbling, drawing, nonphonetic letter strings, invented spellings, and conventional spellings (Sulzby, Teale, & Kamberelis, 1989). Invented spellings are spellings that have meaning to individual children, but that are not consistent with conventional spellings. In the whole language view, children will continue to grow in spelling through modeling by the teacher, instruction, and repeated attempts at spelling until the conventional spelling forms appear (Leu & Kinzer, 1991).

Much of the teacher's role in emergent writing is to encourage, support, and respond to children as they experience writing. Sulzby et al. (1989, p. 77) found that kindergarten teachers who had incorporated writing into their curricula encouraged children to (1) assume ownership of their writing, (2) use writing in their play, (3) use writing in response to other children's writing, (4) share their writing and respond to other children's writing, and (5) use writing to communicate with other people.

In the whole language classroom, teachers may use a variety of strategies to encourage and facilitate students' development of writing skills. Routman (1991) suggested the following components of a "balanced" writing program:

Writing aloud. This is a "powerful modeling technique" in which "the teacher writes in front of students and also verbalizes what he is thinking and writing" (p. 51). The teacher verbalizes all aspects of the writing experience, such as format, spacing, spelling, and vocabulary. Writing is typically done on chart paper, an overhead projector, or a chalkboard, so all students can see and associate what is being written with what is being said.

Shared writing. Using this technique, the teacher and students write collaboratively; the teacher writes on paper as the entire group composes. "In shared writing, the writing is a negotiated process with meanings, choices of words, and topics discussed and decided jointly by students and teacher" (p. 60). The students can focus on composing, since the writing (or scribing) is left to the teacher.

Guided writing. Guided writing is "the heart of the writing program" (p. 66). The student does the writing, and the teacher's role is to "guide students, respond to them, and extend their thinking in the process of composing text" (p. 66). Also, as the need arises, the teacher instructs students in the mechanics or other specific skills, in the context of authentic writing experiences.

Independent writing. With this technique, the student independently uses the writing process without evaluation or intervention by the teacher. "The purpose of independent writing…is to build fluency, establish the writing habit, make personal connections, explore meanings, promote critical thinking, and use writing as a natural, pleasurable, self-chosen activity" (p. 67). Journal writing, a cornerstone activity in whole language programs, is an example of independent writing.

Much of the success of the whole language approach rests with the teacher, who must artfully create an environment in which students feel free to write without any risks and to support and facilitate their efforts. Routman (1991, p. 66) summarized this role by saying: "Teachers are supportive rather than directive, suggestive rather than prescriptive. Ownership of the writing always remains with the student. Our role is to empower writers to discover their own meanings."

Reconsidering the Approaches

If one accepts the essential role of purpose in writing and learning to write, one understands why the strict skills-centered approach to writing instruction is under scrutiny. Students often see little or no value in completing sentences with the correct verb forms, writing fabricated letters, completing "story starters," memorizing lists of words they may not need to use at the time, and so forth. Practicing writing through the use of these strategies "does not produce good writers and, in fact, is not real writing" (Routman, 1991, p. 170). Unfortunately, the traditional approach may lead to students who do not like to write. Calkins (1986, p. 4) explored the role that schools may play in fostering this dislike:

> The bitter irony is that we, in school, set up roadblocks to stifle the natural and enduring reason for writing, and then we complain that our students don't want to write. The cycle continues. After detouring round the authentic, human reasons for writing, we bury the students' urge to write all the more with boxes, kits, and manuals full of synthetic writing-stimulants. At best, they produce artificial and short-lived sputters of enthusiasm for writing, which then fade away, leaving passivity. Worst of all, we accept this passivity as the inevitable context of our teaching.

A meaning-centered approach to writing instruction creates an environment in which students can experience real writing with a real purpose. It bears repeating, however, that it is the *teacher* who initiates and fosters meaning and purpose in the learning environment—not textbooks, teaching manuals, or teaching strategies. Good teaching practices have integrated reading and writing in meaningful contexts (Leu & Kinzer, 1991), and it must be recognized that good teaching has occurred in "traditional" programs.

Teachers probably are most comfortable with an interactive approach to teaching writing, in which meaning and purpose are the main concern, but specific writing skills are considered important for effective written communication. Some teachers believe that writing instruction should focus primarily on meaning, with skills lessons provided, as appropriate, in real and naturally occurring contexts. Other teachers prefer to focus on skills but to ensure that the writing that is completed is meaningful to their students. Whatever approach is used, it is important for teachers to examine the goal of writing—to communicate clearly with an intended audience to achieve a specific purpose—and to ensure that their students are making meaningful progress toward achieving it.

Implications of Approaches to Writing Instruction for Students Who Are Blind

Teachers who work in specialized settings, such as residential schools and self-contained classrooms, as well as teachers in resource room programs who have the primary responsibility for their students' literacy programs, can choose approaches to writing instruction and can structure high-quality learning experiences for students who are blind. These teachers must consider the benefits of the skills-centered approach, the meaning-centered approach, and the interactive approach to teaching writing and make a selection according to the needs of students and the teachers' personal and professional beliefs about literacy learning. One could argue that an interactive approach—which focuses on meaningful and purposeful writing and pays appropriate attention to skills in the context of real writing experiences—would serve the needs of most students who are blind.

However, most special teachers do not have an opportunity to choose one approach over another, since most students who are blind attend integrated programs in their local public schools. In these schools, the regular classroom teachers usually have primary responsibility for writing instruction for students who are blind, and the special teachers provide supplemental instruction and consultation. Regardless of the instructional approach used by the regular classroom teacher, the special teacher must ensure that the student is developing meaningful writing skills, even if he or she has to provide some supplemental instruction.

Supporting Writing Instruction in Skills-Centered Classrooms

In a skills-centered classroom, the regular classroom teacher emphasizes skills, whereas the special teacher focuses on the aspects of writing that are unique in braille, teaching the functional uses of writing and helping the student develop a sense of various audiences. That is, short of influencing the regular teacher's approach to teaching writing, the special teacher maximizes the time spent with the student to ensure that writing tasks are meaningful and relate to life skills.

Supporting Writing Instruction in Meaning-Centered Classrooms

In the meaning-centered classroom, the work of the special teacher is likely to be more demanding and complex than in the skills-centered classroom because regular classroom teachers often capitalize on naturally occurring literacy events and experiences throughout the day, rather than confining writing to a particular time. Therefore, the special teacher must be on hand the entire day to teach the unique aspects of writing in braille as these situations arise. Consider the demands placed on special teachers so students who are blind can gain the full benefits of the writing strategies mentioned earlier by Routman (1991):

- In writing aloud, as the regular teacher writes on an overhead projector or chart paper while verbalizing his or her thoughts on the task, the special teacher *simultaneously* translates into braille what the regular teacher is writing. The special teacher also supplements the regular teacher's comments on format, spelling, and so forth, with information on the unique conventions of the braille code. If the student who is blind only listens to what the regular classroom teacher is saying and waits until a special teacher later provides a braille copy of the story, the value of this "powerful modeling technique" (Routman, 1991, p. 51) is severely minimized or lost entirely.

- In shared writing, students with normal vision can see the immediate effect of their composing processes as the teacher writes the story on a transparency or chalkboard, but a student who is blind has access only to the verbal composing. Again, a special teacher or a certified braille transcriber has to transcribe the story in braille at the same time the teacher is writing it at the front of the class so that the student who is blind can gain the same benefits as classmates with normal vision.

- In guided writing, the regular teacher's guidance at various stages of the writing process is greatly limited because the student is writing in braille. Accessible word processing would provide a direct avenue for guidance by the regular classroom teacher, since print is available on the screen and is output on a printer. However, guidance on aspects of writing by braille is also important, and it must come from a special teacher.

- With independent writing, the student who is blind is on an equal footing with his or her classmates with normal vision because they all are writing without evaluation or intervention by the teacher. Journal writing, a common activity to promote independent writing, can be accomplished easily in braille. The student who is blind may be at a disadvantage when it comes to sharing the work, however, because unless all the students' writing is reproduced on word processors that generate both print and braille copies, all the students will have to read their work out loud. Furthermore, the student who is blind should also have opportunities to share his or her writing with persons who read braille.

As these examples indicate, unless the special teacher is continuously available in a meaning-centered classroom, the student who is blind will not engage in active and valuable learning.

FACILITATING WRITING WITH MICROCOMPUTERS
Microcomputers in General Instruction

The proliferation of microcomputers in schools is changing what students learn and how they learn. Among the many valuable applications of microcomputers and related technologies "in classrooms [is] the freedom they provide young writers through word processing" (Sampson et al., 1991, p. 390).

Word processing frees students from many of the mechanics of writing—penmanship, spelling, punctuation, format, recopying, and so forth—and allows them to concentrate on the message they wish to create and express through writing. Kinzer, Sherwood, and Bransford (1986, pp. 238–239) described the role and benefits of word processing as follows:

> The word processor enables student writers to free short-term memory by concentrating on large-scale revisions of ideas, while holding concerns with spelling and punctuation for later. In addition, having several neatly revised drafts quickly available allows the writer instant feedback on global revisions without the burden of reading through messy corrections and deletions. Having the capability to receive clean copy immediately after revising provides strong, immediate reinforcement. . . . The ease with which complete drafts are provided enables the student writer to see composition as an organic, ongoing process rather than as the hasty production of a complete product. So, writers are encouraged to make global as well as cosmetic revisions at those times when such revisions are most appropriate.

Given the flexibility that word processing provides, it can facilitate the various elements of the writing process (Butler, 1991). Table 6-4 explores some possible implications of microcomputers and word processing for each of the elements in the writing process.

A still-unresolved issue is whether to teach typing or keyboarding skills to students before introducing them to word processing (Kinzer et al., 1986). It may be argued that the hunt-and-peck method gives students immediate access to microcomputers and that requiring them to learn proper keyboarding skills first imposes yet another "mechanical" skill to be mastered that may unnecessarily stifle the writing process. On the other hand, typing teachers would argue that "playing" with the computer keyboard "creates bad typing habits that are almost impossible to erase" (Kinzer et al., 1986, p.239).

Some of the other applications of microcomputers that facilitate writing and writing instruction are as follows:

Drill and Practice Software

Many software programs provide drill in the specific skills of the surface features of writing, such as subject-verb agreement, spelling, and sentence structure. Since these programs attend mainly to the product of writing, not to the process, they may foster bad writing habits, such as failure to make global revisions or lack of fluency in writing (Kinzer et al., 1986, p. 225).

Interactive Software

Butler (1991) noted that a "number of idea-generating programs are designed to help students create characters, plots, settings, and story-lines as a means of composing their own stories [but] as yet there is little evidence as to their effectiveness" (p. 106).

Table 6-4. Implications of the Use of Microcomputers and Word Processing in the Writing Process

Element of the Writing Process	Implications
Prewriting	*To generate topics and ideas for writing activities.* Special interactive software programs can stimulate generation of ideas and topics for writing. Word-processing programs can be used for jotting down thoughts and ideas or for outlining a paper.
Drafting	*To write down initial ideas and thoughts on paper.* Word processing facilitates fluency in writing by bypassing the physical act of forming letters and words and attending to mechanical conventions (such as margins). Since changes in the paper—both revision and editing—can occur efficiently at a later phase in the process, the student is freed to take risks in writing, to be creative, and to search for a personal "voice" or style.
Revision	*To make content changes in the paper.* Word processing facilitates global revisions in writing, allowing the student to add, delete, or move blocks of text of any size. Without the mechanical constraints of recopying, the writer is free to concentrate on the message that is being presented and the audience he or she is trying to affect.
Editing	*To make corrections in spelling, capitalization, usage, etc.* Word processing facilitates editing of papers once content revisions have been made. Errors in capitalization and punctuation are easily made without needing to "recopy" the paper. Spell checkers identify misspelled (or unrecognized) words and offer alternatives. Grammar and style checkers point out possible errors in usage and offer suggestions for changing them.
Publishing	*To prepare one's writing to be shared with a wider audience.* For "public" writing, word processing programs offer a quick, efficient means of printing the final copy of a paper. Simple desk-top publishing features can add graphics, pictures, borders, and so forth to present a "polished" publication.

Electronic Mail and Telecommunications

These systems allow students to communicate or share writing through interconnected computers. Interacting with others through electronic mail allows students to consider the perspectives of others and to develop a sense of audience demands (Kinzer et al., 1986). Such influences, as well as the collaboration involved, can "change the social context for writing" (MacArthur, 1988, p. 541).

Use by Teachers

Teachers can use microcomputers in a variety of ways to facilitate writing instruction. For example, in the language experience approach to reading, rather than write on chart paper, the teacher can use a word processor to record a student's story and then output a clean copy immediately (Leu & Kinzer, 1991). Some software programs analyze the surface features of students' writing products, such as the number of complex sentences and the number of misspelled words. Other programs, such as data bases and filing systems, can handle organizational functions in the classroom (Kinzer et al., 1986).

There is a growing body of research to suggest that microcomputers are valuable in educational interventions, including writing instruction. Also, since more and more jobs are becoming dependent on computers and other technologies, students will need such skills to be competitive in the rapidly changing world of work.

Use of Microcomputers with Students Who Are Blind

Word Processing

Microcomputers that are equipped with special-access technology—speech synthesis devices, braille displays, braille embossers, and so forth—can give students who are blind the same opportunities to use the power of word processors as are provided to all other students. With word processing, students who are blind can

- quickly note ideas, thoughts, or outlines on a given paper
- compose documents with relative ease using the regular keyboard
- monitor and review writing by using speech output or other types of access
- revise work by adding, deleting, or rearranging large blocks of text
- output drafts in braille through grade 2 braille translation software for careful review and more revision, if desired
- edit documents with ease using insertion, deletion, and other functions of the word-processing program, including spell checking and grammar checking in a few programs
- print out final clean copies of their work in print and/or braille.

These characteristics illustrate the power of word processing in facilitating each step in the writing process for students who are blind. Indeed, all the advantages offered to students with normal vision, presented in Table 6-4, are also available to students who are blind if the microcomputer is equipped with special access technology and appropriate software. On a braillewriter or conventional typewriter, the writing process would be significantly restricted, and the entire document would have to be recopied if revisions were made. With accessible word processing, however, most of the work is done while the document is in the computer's memory. If students wish to have a hard copy in braille, they have that option (provided, of course, that a braille embosser is attached to the system).

Research and field experiences have indicated that the mastery of word-processing skills by students who are blind leads to other positive outcomes. Brunken (1984) found that when students used word processing to complete their written assignments, their grades improved 10 percent. Koenig, Mack, Schenk, and Ashcroft (1985) reported that beginning in the fourth grade, students mastered basic applications of braille word processing, given appropriate instruction, and that several high school students independently applied these skills in work experience programs. A field study conducted at the Florida School for the Deaf and Blind found that first-grade students who were blind mastered not only keyboarding skills, but basic word-processing skills and that word-processing skills had a positive impact on the development of the students' reading skills (C. G. Mack, personal communication, 1986).

Other Technologies

Today there are a number of portable notetaking devices that have braille keyboards and store notes and documents in grade 2 braille on a memory board or chip (earlier models of such devices stored information on cassette tapes or 3 1/2-inch computer disks). These devices are easily carried from one place to another, have quiet keyboards, provide speech output (through an earplug, if desired), and can print directly to an inkprint printer and/or a braille embosser. They may also be connected to a microcomputer. Once information is transferred to the microcomputer's memory, the user can take advantage of advanced word-processing capabilities.

One braille notetaker contains a one-cell braille display for editing purposes, and another notetaking device uses a conventional keyboard, rather than a braille keyboard, and provides speech output. Given the flexibility of braille notetakers, it is likely that improvements in them will continue to be made.

Ensuring the Availability of Technology

The educational team is responsible for ensuring that deliberate decisions are made on specific types of technology needed by the student. The team should consider the student's immediate and future literacy needs and the tools required to meet them. Technology specialists from residential schools for students who are blind can assist in assessing the use of specific types of technology to meet the student's needs. Representatives from technology companies can also provide assistance, although it should be recognized that they may have competing interests when recommending technology.

To ensure the appropriate and timely availability of technology, the educational team should make its decisions and place the needed technological devices on the student's individual education plan. Then it becomes the responsibility of the school district to purchase the devices for use by the student in school. Meaningful development of technological skills, however, often will require their use in the home. Since school districts rarely purchase technology for the home, optional funding sources should be explored: family resources, state rehabilitation services for persons who are blind, local community service organizations (such as Lions, Rotary, or Delta Gamma), and so forth.

Ideally, instruction in the use of technological devices will occur far enough in advance that the student is prepared to use them when circumstances dictate. In some instances, the use of a given technological device may be new to the special teacher, especially since new devices are becoming available on a regular basis. The teacher must be skilled in the use of technology to provide appropriate instruction to students, as well as to nurture positive attitudes toward its use as a means of accomplishing literacy and other daily living tasks. If the special teacher is frustrated or perplexed by the use of technology, students, too, will be frustrated or perplexed. A variety of options are available for the teacher to develop technology skills:

- attending special in-service workshops on technology

- studying owner's manuals or other self-instructional materials
- receiving individualized instruction from knowledgeable individuals, such as technology consultants from outreach departments of residential schools or representatives from the manufacturer.

Given the importance of technology in acquiring functional literacy, the teacher must take whatever steps are necessary to gain needed skills and then teach them to his or her students. Preventing the student from learning to use technology because of the teacher's lack of skills would be detrimental to the student's growth in literacy.

TEACHING THE UNIQUE SKILLS OF WRITING TO STUDENTS WHO ARE BLIND

Areas of Unique Need

Special teachers are responsible for teaching, or supporting the teaching of, unique skills to students who are blind. Although writing per se is not unique to students who are blind, the modes of writing—including the use of the braillewriter, slate and stylus, keyboarding, technology, and signature writing—are. Since regular classroom teachers are not skilled in these modes, the special teacher plays a major role in helping students learn them. The unique aspects of the braille code itself—contractions, short-forms words, and composition signs—also require consistent instruction and support by the special teacher, who works collaboratively with the regular classroom teacher to ensure that students who are blind develop meaningful writing skills.

In teaching students who are blind, special teachers need to balance instruction in the tools for writing with meaningful and purposeful writing experiences. For example, a teacher may encourage a student to improve his or her slate-and-stylus skills by having the student label personal tape cassettes or compact discs or make an invitation list to an upcoming birthday party. Since the purpose of both writing tasks is personal and has meaning to the student, the focus is on the functional use of the slate and stylus, rather than solely on the specific mechanics of the device itself.

Because the unique aspect of writing by students who are blind relates to the tools used, special teachers may tend to emphasize the mechanical aspects of writing in braille. For example, especially when students who are blind are placed in an integrated setting, special teachers may perceive that their responsibility is to teach only the unique aspects of writing—the use of the writing tools—and leave the instruction in writing per se to the regular classroom teacher. Thus, they may teach their students to place the paper properly in the brailler, memorize dot numbers, translate dot numbers to keys on the brailler, and so forth, but since these tasks are isolated from the real purposes of writing, the students may see no value in learning them. Or, the special teacher may perceive that teaching the mechanics of writing with a braillewriter or another device or teaching braille contractions *is* teaching writing. This would be similar to teaching a child with normal vision to hold a pencil and expecting that he or she could then write. To avoid either of these misperceptions, the unique skills should always be taught in the context of meaningful and authentic writing experiences.

Another unique aspect of writing by students who are blind is awareness of the receptive medium that an intended audience requires. For example, if the student is writing a letter to a sighted person, print will be the medium to use, not braille. The special teacher helps students who are blind to identify which audiences need to read print and to develop the skills to generate print by applications in real, functional situations, not by lectures or discussions. In Chapter 4 we presented some suggestions for helping students who are blind develop this unique sense of audience.

Writing with a Braillewriter

Most young children who are blind are introduced to writing on the Perkins braillewriter, usually in a school setting. Miller (1985) suggested that if preschoolers who are blind have access to the braillewriter (or a slate and stylus) at home, they will have similar opportunities to "scribble" as do preschoolers with normal vision. However, it should be pointed out that whereas children with normal vision scribble because they are imitating the writing behaviors they have casually observed in their parents or other adults, children who are blind must be given direct opportunities for this "observation" to take place. Therefore, an adult who knows braille should frequently model writing behaviors by placing the child's hands near the embossing head or on the keys while the

The Perkins Brailler

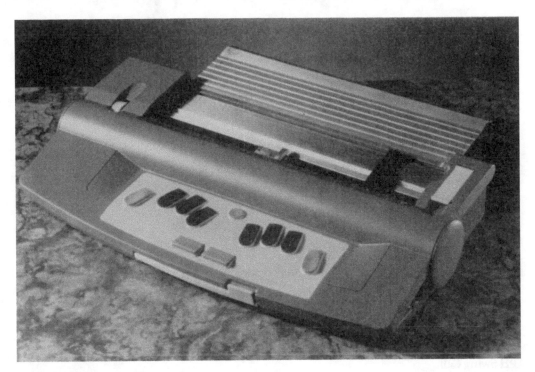

The Mountbatten Brailler

adult is performing real writing tasks, such as writing a letter to Grandma or making a shopping list. Then the child will have true opportunities to imitate this behavior through scribbling.

In teaching young elementary school children the proper character formations on the braillewriter, the special teacher models the movement of the keys with both the student's fingers at the near edge of the keys and the teacher's at the far edge and/or by teaching the child the dot numbers, along with the corresponding keys on the brailler. Such learning should occur while completing meaningful writing tasks, such as writing one's name, making an entry in a journal, or noting the day's weather on a classroom calendar. Drill and practice in forming letters and contractions by themselves is not writing instruction.

APH Swing Cell

The APH Swing Cell was designed to teach the relationship between the dots in a cell and the keys on the brailler. It contains a large braille cell with pegs for each of the dots. The cell is separated down its length and has a hinge on the top of each half. To use the Swing Cell, the student places pegs in the appropriate holes of the cell and then "swings" the hinges up and out to each side. The holes that are filled with pegs then correspond to the keys that should be pressed on the brailler. Early use of the Swing Cell may eliminate the need to rely on memorizing dot numbers in beginning writing instruction because it shows the rela-

APH Swing Cell

tionship between the dots in the braille cell and the keys on the brailler. After a short time, students usually generalize this basic idea to other braille letters or characters.

Conversion to Print

Students in integrated classrooms will have to get work completed on the braillewriter put in an accessible form for the regular classroom teacher. The special teacher or a qualified paraprofessional generally does so through inkprinting or interlining. However, electronic devices are now available that convert grade 2 braille written on the braillewriter immediately into print. As the student hits the line-space key on the braillewriter, an attached printer outputs the information in print. These devices also provide rudimentary formatting and other options (such as output at the end of the page, rather than after each line). The student can then turn in papers to the classroom teacher directly, rather than going through an intermediary process, such as inkprinting. Whether the student's work is interlined or translated via an electronic device, the special teacher can use such processes to help the student understand that most people rely on the use of print.

Writing with a Slate and Stylus

The slate and stylus is a portable tool for writing braille by punching each dot with a metal-tipped stylus on a slate containing indentations of dots in the braille cell. In the conventional slate and stylus, the stylus punches through the paper to form dots on indentations in the slate; therefore, the user moves from right to left in writing. While the use of the slate and stylus has been questioned by some teachers in recent years, the authors of this book maintain that mastery of the slate and stylus is an indispensable skill for persons who are blind and that the issues to be resolved are when to begin instruction in it and how to teach its efficient use.

While some feel that writing should begin with the braillewriter and that the slate and stylus should be introduced between the third and the sixth grade, others believe that the slate and stylus and the braillewriter should be introduced simultaneously and as early as possible. One doesn't teach a sighted child how to use a typewriter and hold back on learning to use a pencil. The early introduction of both the slate and stylus and the braillewriter will ensure a student's proficiency in using both. If a student has been allowed to "scribble" on both, then he or she will be prepared to take on the task of learning to use each as a writing tool.

Students often experience frustration in learning to use the slate and stylus, perhaps because they are reflecting the frustration of their special teachers or because of the teachers' emphasis on the accuracy, rather than on the function, of writing. However, since the slate and stylus is used largely for personal communication, the student's effectiveness in using it should be judged according to his or her ability to communicate with the intended audience, generally, himself or herself. For most tasks requiring the slate and stylus, speed of use and degree of accuracy are functions of the specific task. If the student is taking notes in class, he or she must be fast enough to record the essential information provided by the teacher, but must be accurate enough to read the notes later to study for a test. If the student is too slow because of an overriding concern for accuracy, then important information may be missed. If the task is to jot down a telephone number, then accuracy is required.

Instruction in use of the slate and stylus provides an excellent opportunity to focus the student's attention on the receptive communication demands of an audience. If the student

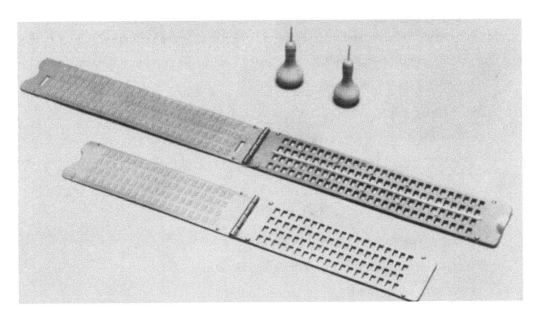

Examples of slates and styli

is the audience, such as when taking notes in class or making personal lists, then he or she is free to write with whatever level of accuracy is needed to read the information back later. If the audience is another individual who knows braille, such as a special teacher or a friend who is blind, then the accuracy must increase to a level that will match the expectations of the audience. (See the accompanying suggestions for teaching the effective use of the slate and stylus; for detailed instructions, see Mangold, 1985.)

Writing by Typing and Keyboarding

There is widespread agreement that students who are blind need to master touch-typing skills because typing allows direct communication through written language with persons who read print. Traditionally, students who are blind were introduced to touch typing on typewriters around the third grade. However, with students' success in using microcomputers, many professionals now advocate introducing touch typing on a microcomputer keyboard, rather than on a typewriter. Keyboarding skills are facilitated by microcomput-

---

SUGGESTIONS FOR TEACHING WRITING WITH THE SLATE AND STYLUS

- Develop in the student an understanding of the value and uses of the slate and stylus through modeling prior to beginning instruction (for example, teacher uses slate and stylus to jot down feedback and grade on test).

- Use a hand-over-hand method to introduce mechanics of forming characters and contractions with the slate and stylus. Some teachers may prefer to use dot-number formations if this is the way the student learned to write with a braillewriter.

- Avoid unnecessary drill and practice in forming characters and contractions. Place emphasis on communicative effectiveness and the efficiency with which successful communication takes place.

- Begin using the slate and stylus for functional writing purposes as soon as possible:

   ✔ jotting down homework assignments

   ✔ writing note to teacher of the visually handicapped

   ✔ making personal list, such as, things to get at K-Mart

   ✔ labeling personal items, such as compact discs, cassettes, clothes

   ✔ writing name and telephone number of a friend

   ✔ taking notes in a class

   ✔ jotting short note or letter to a blind friend

   ✔ signing a birthday card or other greeting cards

   ✔ writing recipes and labeling canned goods.

(continued on next page)

ers that are equipped with speech synthesis devices that allow for immediate feedback on what the student has typed, thereby presenting a significant advantage over the traditional typewriter.

Earlier, there was a brief discussion on the issue of allowing students with normal vision to hunt and peck on the microcomputer keyboard before they are taught formal keyboarding skills. This issue is not pertinent in the field of blindness, however: Keyboarding skills are a necessary prerequisite for using a microcomputer for students who are blind (Mack & Koenig, 1991).

Despite the success of first graders reported earlier, as yet there is insufficient research to support a specific recommendation on when to introduce keyboarding skills to young children who are blind. The most reasonable approach is to base decisions on individual abilities with consistent diagnostic assessment beginning as early as kindergarten. Teachers can work cooperatively with young children to develop an awareness of microcomputers, using simple computer programs with speech output, such as games or listening activities, that

---

- Incorporate use of the slate and stylus throughout the school day and into the evening. Start with tasks that do not require a high degree of accuracy (such as making personal lists) and move toward those that do require accuracy (for example, jotting down a telephone number).

- As instruction advances, place emphasis on developing speed for note-taking purposes. Prior instruction in note taking on the braillewriter is necessary. Again, avoid overemphasis on accuracy.

- Practice note-taking skills from a cassette recording of a class lecture.

- Discuss with the student the difference between writing for personal uses in which accuracy and neatness are judged by the writer himself or herself and writing for others in which accuracy and neatness are judged by others.

- Discuss with the student the tasks for which the slate and stylus should be used and those tasks for which another mode of writing is more appropriate. For example, a computer word-processing program would be more appropriate for completing a term paper.

- Reinforce student's appropriate selection of one mode of writing over other options. If an inappropriate selection of a writing mode is made, use problem-solving techniques with the student to gain an appreciation for use of an alternative mode.

- Incorporate study of grade 3 braille and/or personal contractions for note taking with the slate and stylus as student progresses into high school.

- Familiarize the student with a variety of different types of slate and stylus instruments and their uses (for example, one-liner for labeling).

require minimal keyboarding skills. When teachers find that their students are able to type in simple commands, first with physical guidance and then independently—with fingers maintained on the home row keys—then they have justification for introducing a keyboarding program. Fortunately, a variety of programs that provide auditory output through speech synthesis devices can be used to teach keyboarding skills. Since some of these programs are designed for the general population, their cost is modest.

As with all writing skills, students must see a purpose in developing keyboarding skills. Although interest may be sustained for a time by games and gimmicks—such as "shooting" letters, in one popular software program—children must consider keyboarding a means to a purposeful end. Therefore, it is essential to move them as expediently as possible to meaningful writing activities. The best way to provide such opportunities is through word processing, which is discussed next.

Writing with Microcomputer Word Processing

Word processing is an indispensable skill for students who are blind. When appropriate access technology and software are used, word processing provides an easy and efficient means of writing. Documents created by microcomputer word processors can be output in print or braille, so communication is facilitated both through braille for the individual who is blind and through print for others who have normal vision. Since few would disagree with the need to teach students who are blind to use accessible word processing, the questions relate to when and how to teach word-processing skills.

Ideally, a student should begin word processing as soon as his or her keyboarding skills are developed to the extent that rudimentary control of the computer is possible. Students who use touch keyboarding to locate the letter keys, return keys, delete key, space bar, and control keys accurately are likely to be ready for instruction in word processing. Their use of word processing for writing meaningful discourse will undoubtedly increase their accuracy through practice and through the immediate feedback they receive from the access devices and the teacher. Delaying instruction in word processing may interfere with the student's appreciation of the value of keyboarding skills and may prevent the student from enjoying the many benefits of word processing.

The special teacher will find few resources and instructional materials for teaching word processing skills to his or her students. The instructions are usually geared toward teaching the teacher to use access devices and accessible software and may not be appropriate for the students. Therefore, the teacher may find it necessary to consult specialists in technology at residential schools for students with visual impairments for assistance in learning adaptive equipment and software and teaching skills to their students.

The special teacher should master and feel comfortable with the word-processing program and access technology before instructing students. Generally, individualized instruction with the student is the most appropriate method, with the teacher providing verbal guidance throughout the various steps in the process and gradually fading the cues as the student becomes increasingly independent. An informal checklist of essential skills and commands in using a specific word processor (see Koenig et al., 1985, for example) may serve both a curricular and an evaluative function.

A word of caution is once again necessary. Given the "mechanics" of using microcomputers and word processing programs, it is easy to focus on the mechanical skills rather than on writing. The word processor is only a means to the end: the successful communication of a message to an intended audience. Since word processing allows direct communication with individuals who read print, all the purposes of writing presented in Table 6-1 can be accomplished by accessible word processors for students who are blind.

Handwriting Skills

At some point during the school years, students who are blind will learn some basic handwriting skills, although these are generally confined to signature writing. Signature writing is used primarily for signing checks and legal documents, as well as letters and other forms of personal communication. To address the functionality of signature writing, it is ideal to begin instruction before the student plans to open a checking account.

To teach signature writing, special teachers often make thermoform patterns of their students' names that the students use to practice forming and connecting letters. They also may order instructional materials on cursive letter formations and raised-line paper for their students' use from the American Printing House for the Blind. Another alternative is to follow Weis and Weis's (1978) unique approach for teaching cursive writing skills to persons who are congenitally blind by using the spatial arrangement and dot-numbering pattern of the braille cell to guide letter formations. For example, when making a capital A, the student is told to start at dot 3, then go to dot 1, to dot 4, to dot 1, to dot 3, to dot 6, to dot 4, and back to dot 6 and then to connect to dot 3 of the adjoining cell (or another dot depending on the next letter). The effect is a type of "squarehand," but the student can learn to curve the edges after mastering the basic formations.

It is uncommon for students who are blind to go much beyond signature writing in handwriting skills. However, the authors have seen adults who are blind use manuscript-writing skills to write short notes to friends who are sighted or to jot down phone numbers for others. One author worked with a junior high school student who had developed sufficient manuscript-writing skills at an early age to complete assignments that she presented directly to her regular classroom teachers. Despite these individual successes, the authors recommend that the educational team should consider the value of other writing tools, especially technology that provides print output, as priorities over manuscript-writing skills.

Spelling Skills and Braille Contractions

The braille code influences the development of spelling and writing skills in two ways. First, the student learns that words in braille are written with various contractions and short forms, as well as other conventions (such as capital dots). For students who are congenitally blind, using the unique features of the braille code is *the* way to write, since the various conventions of the print code are unknown at the early stages. Second, the student learns to "spell out" (or learns uncontracted versions) of words in spelling. In classrooms that have spelling textbooks, the traditional approach is to have students use both contracted and uncontracted versions of words in the spelling lists; when both versions are written accurately, the word is considered "correct."

The special teacher should always remember that the goal of writing is to communicate. Students learn to write as they use written language for the purpose of communication. Therefore, the most meaningful way to learn the unique aspects of braille is to infuse such instruction in authentic writing experiences. Consider the following ways in which Routman's (1991) meaning-centered writing strategies can be used to introduce students naturally to contractions, short forms, and braille conventions:

In writing aloud, the special teacher emphasizes the meaning by composing the piece of writing while verbalizing each aspect of the experience. Then he or she may cycle back through the piece to verbalize the appropriate use of braille conventions. The teacher may also draw attention to the receptive demands of the audience and verbalize the process of deciding on the appropriate form for this writing task.

In shared writing, the special teacher verbalizes the use of braille conventions as they naturally occur. There is no reason to fabricate sentences with certain contractions or short forms, since they will simply appear in words that the student is using. If certain braille forms do not appear, the teacher should question whether it is important for the student to know them at that time.

In guided writing, the special teacher's provision of ongoing guidance presents natural opportunities to use contractions and short forms within the context of a meaningful writing experience. Since the student has read books in standard braille and heard the teacher model the use of various contractions and short forms while using writing aloud and shared writing, those forms will likely be used when the student is in control of the scribing process. If not, the teacher provides guidance in their use as the need arises.

In independent writing, the special teacher does not (and should not) provide guidance or feedback on appropriate braille conventions, since the purpose of independent writing is to promote self-expression and pleasure in writing. Therefore, when the student uses some "invented" and misspelled words or violates some braille conventions, the teacher does not correct the student. In responding to independent writing in a meaning-centered manner, the teacher reacts to the meaning presented in the writing, *not* to surface-level features like spelling and capitalization.

If the special teacher focuses writing instruction on the specific conventions of the braille code, attention is diverted from the communicative function of writing. Furthermore, the student may come to believe that writing is a tedious undertaking whose purpose is to get "all the dots right."

The use of microcomputer word-processing and notetaking devices provides natural ways to learn the unique aspects of braille. Uncontracted versions of words are typically used in word processing, so this is a meaningful time to learn the spelled-out forms of words (in contrast to spelling lists in traditional programs). Braille notetaking devices allow students to input in contracted braille; when the space bar is pressed, a speech synthesizer voices the word (if it is directed to do so). If a correct braille form was not used, the voiced version of the word provides this feedback. The development of meaningful writing is facilitated with microcomputers and notetakers through any of the writing strategies just discussed.

SUMMARY

This chapter has explored two different approaches to writing instruction. The traditional approach views writing as a product of a collection of discrete skills that are often taught in isolation. The expectation (or hope) is that the student will integrate and generalize the fragmented skills into mature writing. In contrast, the meaning-centered approach views writing as a recursive and dynamic process in which the meaning, purpose, and value of writing serve as guiding principles. Writing and other language processes are taught—or their growth is facilitated—holistically, and specific skills are introduced when the need arises. Microcomputer applications, especially word processing, are valuable ways to facilitate the writing process for students and writing instruction for teachers.

Teachers of students who are blind provide support and supplemental instruction in unique skills in classrooms that use a variety of approaches to writing instruction. The overriding goal is to help students develop the cadre of writing skills that will provide the foundation for effective written communication throughout life.

As highly specialized professionals within the field of special education, teachers of students who are blind have much to learn from experienced and knowledgeable "regular" educators like Calkins and Routman. Calkins (1986, p. 9) referred to the teaching of writing as an art, suggesting that teachers "must remember that it is not the number of good ideas that turns our work into art, but the selection, balance and design of those ideas." And Routman (1991, p. 194) surely agreed when she wrote: "I no longer believe that writing can be taught. The best we can do as teachers is to nurture writing, encourage it, sustain it, and give it time, space, freedom, and room in which to grow."

REFERENCES

Atwell, N. (1987). *In the middle: Writing, reading, and learning with adolescents.* Upper Montclair, NJ: Boynton/Cook.

Brunken, P. (1984). Independence for the visually handicapped through technology. *Education of the Visually Handicapped, 15,* 127-133.

Butler, S. (1991). The writing connection. In V. Froese (Ed.), *Whole-language: Practice and theory* (pp. 97–147). Boston: Allyn & Bacon.

Calkins, L. M. (1986). *The art of teaching writing.* Portsmouth, NH: Heinemann.

DeGroff, L. J. C., & Leu, D. J. (1987). An analysis of writing activities: A study of language arts textbooks. *Written Communication, 4,* 253–268.

Farnan, N., Lapp, D., & Flood, J. (1992). Changing perspectives in writing instruction. *Journal of Reading, 35,* 550–556.

Graves, D. H. (1983). *Writing: Teachers and children at work.* Portsmouth, NH: Heinemann.

Graves, D. H. (1984). *A researcher learns to write: Selected articles and monographs.* Portsmouth, NH: Heinemann.

Harp, B. (1991). Principles of assessment and evaluation in whole language classrooms. In B. Harp (Ed.), *Assessment and evaluation in whole language programs* (pp. 35–50). Norwood, MA: Christopher-Gordon.

Kinzer, C. K., Sherwood, R. D., & Bransford, J. D. (1986). *Computer strategies for education: Foundations and content area applications.* Columbus, OH: Charles E. Merrill.

Koenig, A. J., Mack, C. G., Schenk, W. A., & Ashcroft, S. C. (1985). Developing writing and word processing skills with visually impaired children: A beginning. *Journal of Visual Impairment & Blindness, 79,* 308–310; 312.

Leu, D. J., & Kinzer, C. K. (1991). *Effective reading instruction, K-8* (2nd ed.). New York: Merrill.

MacArthur, C. A. (1988). The impact of computers on the writing process. *Exceptional Children, 54,* 536–542.

Mack, C. G., & Koenig, A. J. (1991). *Access to technology for students with visual handicaps.* Reston, VA: Council for Exceptional Children, Division on Visual Handicaps.

Mangold, P. N. (1985). Teaching the braille slate and stylus: A manual for mastery. Castro Valley, CA: Exceptional Teaching Aids.

Miller, D. D. (1985). Reading comes naturally: A mother and her blind child's experiences. *Journal of Visual Impairment & Blindness, 79,* 1–4.

Noyce, R. M., & Christie, J. F. (1989). *Integrating reading and writing instruction in grades K-8.* Boston: Allyn & Bacon.

Routman, R. (1988). *Transitions: From literature to literacy.* Portsmouth, NH: Heinemann.

Routman, R. (1991). *Invitations: Changing as teachers and learners K–12.* Portsmouth, NH: Heinemann.

Sampson, M., Van Allen, R., & Sampson, M. B. (1991). *Pathways to literacy.* Fort Worth: Holt, Rinehart, & Winston.

Sulzby, E., Teale, W. H., & Kamberelis, G. (1989). Emergent writing in the classroom: Home and school connections. In D. S. Strickland & L. M. Morrow (Eds.), *Emerging literacy: Young children learn to read and write* (pp. 63–79). Newark, DE: International Reading Association.

Weis, J., & Weis, J. (1978). Teaching handwriting to the congenitally blind. *Journal of Visual Impairment & Blindness, 72,* 280–283.

Yatvin, J. (1981). A functional writing program for the middle grades. In S. Haley-James (Ed.), *Perspectives on writing in grades 1–8* (pp. 43–57). Urbana, IL: National Council of Teachers of English.

ASSESSMENT OF BRAILLE LITERACY

Approaches for assessing literacy are changing, along with the infusion of meaning-centered approaches to literacy instruction. The reliance on standardized tests of reading and writing is being supplemented by or replaced with "authentic" assessment that occurs within the natural context of literacy learning. Instead of relying on test scores to judge students' progress in literacy, teachers are using more informal, but qualitatively more meaningful strategies, such as having students retell stories, write journals, or evaluate themselves; observing students during the writing process; interviewing students on their reading and writing experiences; and using informal literacy checklists and criterion-referenced inventories. Such strategies empower teachers as the individuals who are the most qualified to measure the students' growth in literacy.

In some respects, authentic assessment may be considered more an art than a science, in contrast to the use of formal measures like standardized tests. Froese (1991) suggested that a meaning-centered assessment should

- be holistic rather than fragmented,
- be student centered or cooperative, rather than only teacher centered,
- focus on the process of writing, not only the product,
- combine teaching and assessment, rather than separate them,
- use teachers' observations and assessment, rather than standardized tests,
- occur over time, rather than at an arbitrary point.

The need for changes in the assessment of literacy was reflected also in *Becoming a Nation of Readers* (Anderson, Hiebert, Scott, & Wilkinson, 1985). This highly influential report suggested three needed areas of reform in current measures of assessment:

1. Less emphasis should be placed on *formal assessment measures* that are designed to measure discrete reading skills in isolation, apart from classroom instruction. Critics

maintain that formal assessment measures are not valid indicators of classroom literacy learning and real-life applications.

2. New *process assessment measures* need to be developed that reflect current views of reading as a constructive, interactive, strategic, and holistic process. Such measures should assess the application of these processes while the students are learning information from authentic, content-specific texts.

3. More *informal classroom assessment measures* and observations need to be designed that reflect and document the development of students as language learners (reading, writing, listening, and speaking) within authentic learning contexts.

Issues of assessment generally plague teachers of students who are blind, the students themselves, their parents, and others on the education team. No one ever seems pleased with the results of assessments, primarily because they leave more questions unanswered than answered and because they often do not seem to be applicable in planning programs of students who are blind. Perhaps more alarming, it seems as though little is done to address the complexities of assessment other than delineating the problems. Therefore, given the changes that are occurring in both literacy instruction and general programming for students who are blind, it is essential that more meaningful and authentic assessments are devised for evaluating the literacy of blind children, so that the results can be used to improve the quality of the children's lives.

This chapter discusses various types of assessment—formal and informal—and explores their applications for assessing the growth in literacy of students who are blind. Although a great deal of attention is paid to standardized assessment, it is only for addressing concerns about their use and suggesting the need to balance standardized tests with other sources of authentic assessment information. This chapter concludes with a framework for the meaningful assessment of literacy that is used in meaning-centered classrooms.

STANDARDIZED LITERACY TESTS

Description

Standardized tests are the most widely used type of formal assessment in the United States today. Regardless of the instructional approaches used to teach literacy—basal series, language experience, literature based, or whole language—nearly every school district administers some type of standardized test yearly throughout the elementary grades. These norm-referenced tests compare a child's performance with the average performances of other "like" children in the norming group or reference group (such as third graders or 17 year olds). Norms are established on the basis of the performance of representative, nationwide samples of children in each grade.

Standard scores from norm-referenced tests are typically reported as grade-equivalent scores and/or percentile scores. For example, if Mary is reading at a 2.7 grade-equivalent level, it appears that she is reading at the level an average second grader would be reading after seven months of instruction. Or, if she is reading at the 91st percentile level, she is reading better than 91 out of 100 second graders. Regardless of the type of standard score used, half the children who are tested will score above average and half will score below average.

At a minimum, most standardized reading tests contain vocabulary and comprehension subtests and may contain other reading skills subtests. Vocabulary subtests typically include multiple-choice questions that require matching isolated terms with "correct" definitions in a "one correct answer" format. Comprehension subtests usually contain a series of short reading passages, followed by a series of "one correct answer" multiple-choice questions. Standardized tests of writing generally use multiple-choice questions that direct students to examine, for example, several spellings of a word and select the appropriate spelling or several sentences and identify the one containing a grammatical error. Charney (1984, p. 66) stated that such tests assess "the student's ability to distinguish between standard and nonstandard English, or their ability to choose the most 'correct' or the most 'mature' alternative to a defective construction."

Criticisms

There has been ample criticism of norm-referenced tests, often directed at their lack of validity. On the one hand, Harp (1991) stated without reservation that these tests were of no help to teachers, and Anderson et al. (1985) noted that standardized tests of reading comprehension manifestly do not measure everything required to understand and appreciate a novel, learn from a science book, or find items in a catalog. On the other hand, Gere, Fairbanks, Howes, Roop, and Schaafsma (1992, p. 249) suggested that although "standardized scores may occasionally provide useful information for teachers," teacher-developed measures probably would be more useful. Clearly, the use of norm-referenced tests to assess writing is consumed in the more global issues of appropriate and meaningful assessment.

The increasing pressure for accountability reinforces the continued use of formal standardized tests, since these tests yield norm-referenced numerical data that are used to compare (or rank order from the highest scores to the lowest scores) individual students, whole classes in a building or a school district, schools within a district, or school districts in a state; they are also used for comparisons among states, regions, and even nations, as evidenced by recent literacy studies at the international level (see Figure 7-1). Standardized tests are sometimes used to measure teachers' instructional effectiveness.

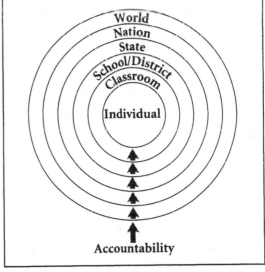

Figure 7-1. Levels of Assessment Accountability

Problems in Use of Standardized Tests with Students Who Are Blind

Concerns over the use of standardized assessments are magnified when the needs of students who are blind are considered. Some typical concerns are listed in "Using Standardized Tests with Students Who Are Blind."

Adapting Tests

A multitude of problems are caused by adapting standardized tests in braille or tactual form. When any standardized procedure is modified in any way, the test is rendered invalid. Therefore, modifications like a simple transcription from print to braille and substituting raised-line figures for print charts and graphs will violate the validity of a standardized test. Commonly used modifications, such as describing pictures that were omitted in a braille version or reading passages aloud to students, may actually change the specific skill that is measured by the test—from reading to listening.

Omitting Items

Omitting items or sections from the braille version of the test affects both validity and reliability. Validity is affected because the test no longer measures the complete sample of skills or behaviors of the print version of the test, and reliability is affected because the test is shorter after items are omitted. Generally, publishers of standardized tests put just enough items in a test to get the desired level of reliability; thus, when items are omitted, the reliability of the test decreases.

Differences in Acculturation

Another major problem in the use of these tests relates to the possible differences in acculturation of students who are blind and students who have normal vision. Acculturation is a "set of background experiences in educational, social, and cultural environments" (Salvia & Ysseldyke, 1988, p. 14). At the very least, students who are blind have a different sensory basis for the experiences they bring to the educational setting and do not have access to some experiences that are purely visual phenomena (such as distance perspective and color). Furthermore, some blind students simply lack basic life experiences because of the overprotectiveness of caregivers and/or the lack of opportunity to encounter a full range of experiences. To make nondiscriminatory use of a norm-referenced test, students who are blind would need to have similar levels of acculturation as their peers in the norming sample. However, it is difficult to establish a criterion for the level of acculturation with students who are blind.

Practical Utility

In addition to significant problems related to reliability and validity, there are more important problems of practical utility. How does one begin to use percentile ranks, grade equivalents, stanine scores, and so forth as a basis for planning an educational program? Norm-referenced, standardized tests of reading and writing were never intended to guide a teacher on what to do with students at a specific time; rather, they were designed to compare the skills of an individual student with those in a certain referent group, generally in a certain age or grade category. Nor were such tests designed to provide information for planning goals and objectives for students. In fact, most questions that teachers have about a student's literacy growth are answered by other types of assessments, not by standardized tests.

USING STANDARDIZED TESTS WITH STUDENTS WHO ARE BLIND

PROBLEMS IN ADAPTING TESTS

- Any modification in a test will violate the standard procedures established by the test's publisher. Therefore, validity and reliability are likely to be affected.

- The degree of acculturation of students who are blind may be different from that of students with normal vision.

- A modified test item may change the skill or task being assessed.

- Some items on tests may not be appropriate for students who are blind.

- The modified test may not match the curriculum being used by the school.

- The elimination of items will affect the reliability of the test.

- If test items are eliminated, certain skills areas are likely to be underrepresented.

- Adapted norm-referenced tests are often used to answer assessment questions when other types of test would be more appropriate.

- As a sole source of assessment data, scores on an achievement test do not provide adequate information for instructional programming.

PROBLEMS IN DEVELOPING AND NORMING TESTS

- The population of students who are blind does not approach a normal distribution.

- It would be difficult or impossible to select a representative sample of students who are blind.

- It would be difficult or impossible to acquire an adequate sample size at each age or grade level for norming the test.

- A variety of factors influence performance, such as the age at onset of blindness, level of vision, and presence of multiple disabilities.

- Given the foregoing problems, norms would lack meaning. Furthermore, how would information be used for programming?

- Special norms would answer the questions, "How does this student compare to other students with visual impairments?" Is this the question teachers generally want to answer?

Table 7-1 presents some typical questions that teachers may have about students and the types of assessments that may provide the appropriate answers.

With all the problems related to modifying standardized tests, especially issues of acculturation, some may wonder why tests are not designed and normed specifically for students who are blind. This approach raises another set of concerns, which are outlined in the box on page 115. Foremost would be the difficulty of getting a "representative" sample of students who are blind, since they are few in number and have diverse learning characteristics. Such tests would allow for comparisons with other students who were blind of the same age or grade and perhaps levels of acculturation. However, the major comparison that is most often desired is generally with students in a regular classroom serving as the referent group; that is, "How does this student who is blind compare with peers in the same classroom with normal vision?" Also, there are questions of how specially designed and normed tests would be used. Since the trend is generally away from norm-referenced tests, it is unlikely that there will be any concerted effort to design and norm tests for students who are blind in the future.

Table 7-1. Matching Assessment Questions to Assessment Tools

Questions	Assessment Tools
What sight words does Thomas identify automatically?	Criterion-referenced checklist
Did Areanna learn all the reading skills presented in this unit?	Curriculum-based inventory
What elements of the writing process does Patrick use effectively?	Classroom observation
Why is Marietta having difficulty comprehending stories in her basal reader?	Diagnostic teaching
What braille contractions does Frank need to learn to use properly in his writing?	Error analysis (from writing sample)
Does Patricia have adequate experiences to support reading and writing experiences presented in the classroom?	Interview with student Interview with parent Observation in home and in the community
In what aspects of accessible word processing does Mark need additional instruction and/or practice?	Criterion-referenced checklist
Does Tina use context cues to attack unknown words in reading?	Observation during reading Miscue analysis Cloze procedure
Is Matthew's reading level comparable to that of his peers with normal vision?	Curriculum-based inventories Norm-referenced test (plus other supporting information)
Is Matthew socially prepared to enter a regular public school classroom?	Observation checklist Behavior rating scale

Despite the problems associated with using standardized tests, these tests still represent one of the most common attempts to measure literacy for students who are blind. If the purpose for the assessment guided the selection of assessment instruments and techniques, standardized tests would rarely be used. As Table 7-1 indicated, teachers rarely wish to know the information provided by standardized tests. The types of questions teachers have about their students' literacy growth are more readily answered by other types of assessment procedures and techniques. When a standardized test is needed to answer a specific question about how the student compares with other students at the same grade or age level, then the results of norm-referenced tests should always be supplemented with a wealth of information from informal assessments (described later). Some suggestions for using standardized tests—when they are determined to be necessary—are listed in the accompanying guidelines.

PROCESS ASSESSMENT

More and more states have developed or are developing assessments that measure the constructive, interactive, strategic, and holistic aspects of the reading process in authentic, content-specific text passages. One model of this type of process assessment is the Illinois Goal Assessment Program's (IGAP) state-wide reading assessment (*Assessing Reading in Illinois*, 1988).

SOME GUIDELINES FOR THE USE
OF STANDARDIZED TESTS WITH STUDENTS WHO ARE BLIND

- Use standardized, norm-referenced tests only when there is a specific need to compare the relative standing of a student who is blind with peers who have normal vision.

- If there is not a specific need to make such a comparison, use other assessment tools.

- When a standardized test is required to answer an appropriate assessment question, use only a test that

    ✔ has established validity and reliability before any modification

    ✔ has been rigorously and professionally modified

    ✔ has had norms adjusted, if necessary, to reflect omitted items

    ✔ will address the skill area of interest.

- When using any standardized test, support the validity of results with other sources of assessment data.

- In any assessment of a student with a confirmed or suspected visual impairment, the teacher of students with visual impairment, the diagnostician, and other members of the educational team must work collaboratively to ensure a valid assessment.

The IGAP reading assessment is organized into four subtests that are consistent with recent theories of the reading process: (1) "Topic Familiarity" (schema theory), (2) "Construction Meaning" (constructive, interactive process), (3) "Reading Strategies" (strategic, metacognitive process), and (4) "Literacy Experiences" (literacy learning). Students within each grade level that is tested (grades 3, 6, 8, or 10) read three authentic, whole-text passages involving both narrative and expository discourse. After reading each passage, they respond to items that may have one, two, or three acceptable answers. "Constructing meaning" items involve interacting with text passages at a text-explicit (literal), text-implicit (interpretive), or schema-implicit (applied) level.

INFORMAL CLASSROOM ASSESSMENTS

Informal classroom assessment methods, such as teacher-made tests and behavioral checklists, are those that do not adhere to strict standardized procedures. Teachers use these methods regularly to judge students' mastery of skills that are being taught in the classroom and to plan future lessons. Such informal techniques are never norm referenced because the intent is not to compare one student to other students, but to determine what skills an individual student demonstrates or does not demonstrate.

A variety of assessment strategies encompass both reading and writing. These strategies are consistent with the movement toward whole language learning—since instruction integrates both reading and writing, so will the assessment strategies in many cases. Portfolio assessment, criterion-referenced tests, conferences, and observation are described next, as are strategies that are specific to reading (miscue analysis and cloze procedures) or writing (holistic scoring, analytic scales, and atomistic measures). The discussion that follows represents a brief glimpse of some of the informal assessment strategies, but by no means is inclusive.

Portfolio Assessment

Perhaps the most dramatic recent change in the informal classroom assessment of students has been the growing use of portfolio assessment by teachers in both whole language and traditional classrooms. The use of portfolios in assessment involves collecting and/or recording samples of students' language performances, products, and behaviors "on an ongoing basis and examining [them] for evidence of literacy growth" (Leu & Kinzer, 1991, p. 471). Portfolios help parents understand the continuous development of their child's literacy skills; show students how their literacy skills have grown; and help teachers identify the students' strengths and weaknesses and develop appropriate literacy experiences to ensure their continued growth.

Portfolios may contain any of the following:

- scores on informal classroom tests
- scores on formal tests
- samples of students' writing

- a list of the number and nature of books read independently
- checklists of reading and writing behaviors and performances
- responses to inventories of attitudes and interests
- students' evaluations of their own performance
- anecdotal records of teachers concerning students' behaviors, performance, and progress
- favorite entries from students' writing journals
- results from informal reading inventories
- results of oral miscue analyses.

Assessments are conducted through the careful examination, discussion, and reflection of the writing contained in the portfolio, often in interactive conferences between the student and teacher. Although the concept is sound, Routman (1991) expressed concerns that portfolios may become merely "collection silos" that do not serve any real purpose. Thus, it is important to maintain a focus on the portfolio as "a dynamic entity that is continually modified and clearly reflects ongoing progress, [not as] a repository of work waiting to be graded" (Leu & Kinzer, 1991, p. 474).

Observation

Routman (1991, p. 303) considers observation to be "the most critical component in evaluation." A variety of specific tools can be used to facilitate observations, including anecdotal records and checklists. Anecdotal records, which Sampson, Van Allen, and Sampson (1991, p. 257) believe are the "cornerstone of the assessment program in meaning-centered classrooms," are ongoing records of what is happening in the classrooms as related to individual students. Informal checklists can serve as a record of skills that have been mastered, are emerging, or are not present. With checklists, however, the teacher may tend to focus on the list of skills to be checked, rather than on what the student is doing (Routman, 1991). Observations and diligent record keeping provide the teacher with information on areas of strength and needed improvements and document growth in reading and writing over time.

Conferences

Conferences of students and teachers serve a variety of functions in the meaning-centered classroom, only one of which is to evaluate growth in reading and writing. The connection between assessment and teaching in meaning-centered classrooms, noted earlier, is clearly evident here, since the various types of conferences overlap (Calkins, 1986).

In evaluation conferences, the student and teacher review the student's reading and writing—perhaps contained in a portfolio—and together explore the student's interests, strengths, needs, goals for instruction, future writing projects, and so forth. The teacher also may use the conference to teach one or two needed skills that have been identified (Tierney, Carter, & Desai, 1991). In writing conferences, it is essential for the teacher to facilitate and reinforce the students' ability to evaluate themselves. Having students take charge of their own literacy learning and actively engage in self-evaluation are high priorities in the meaning-centered classroom (Sampson et al., 1991).

Criterion-Referenced Measures

Criterion-referenced tests are used in schools that teach a published set of sequential reading skills and use different levels of materials that progressively increase in difficulty. The child's scores on tests are compared to predetermined criterion levels (or mastery levels, performance levels, competency levels, and the like) to determine whether the child has mastered a certain skill or set of skills or whether the child is ready to move on to the next level of instructional materials. A publisher of a textbook series provides a curriculum-based inventory for the specific purpose of measuring progress in that series. The criterion tests that accompany *Patterns: The Primary Braille Reading Program* are examples of criterion-based inventories.

For students who are blind, the use of criterion-referenced measures provides a valuable way to assess progress in a chosen textbook series or other published program. Since these are informal measures, there are no problems with violating standardized procedures. Of course, to ensure the validity of criterion-referenced measures, the special teacher must adapt them in meaningful ways to make sure that they measure the skills in question. For example, if a criterion-referenced measure is intended to measure narrative reading skills, then the teacher should transcribe the passage in braille, as well as any accompanying exercises. If the special teacher chose to read the passage aloud to the student to complete the exercises, then listening skills—not reading skills—would be assessed.

Appropriately modified criterion-referenced tests will pinpoint the skills needed for instruction. They yield no unnecessary comparisons with classmates or statistics. Criterion-referenced measures simply identify skills that are not present or skills that need to be developed at a higher level of mastery. If there is a criticism of criterion-referenced measures, it may be that they tend to separate holistic processes, such as reading and writing, into a number of subskills. Both the regular classroom teacher and the special teacher should work collaboratively to make sure that the student is developing meaningfully integrated literacy skills, not a collection of isolated or fragmented subskills.

Miscue Analysis

Miscue analysis is an informal assessment strategy that is used to gain qualitative information about a student's oral reading skills. The term *miscue* is used, rather than *error* (which generally denotes that something is wrong), since not all miscues are harmful to the reading process. Miscue analysis focuses on the qualitative information provided by miscues, rather than on the simple counting of errors or the calculation of error rates or correct reading rates.

In analyzing miscues, the teacher attempts to determine the type of language information—graphophonemic, semantic, or syntactic—the reader used in making the miscues. In the ideal pattern of language usage in reading, a balance is maintained among the three types of information.

Procedures for analyzing miscues range from the complex (see, for example, Goodman & Burke, 1972) to the simple (for example, Christie, 1979). Although teachers are less likely to understand and use complex procedures, they can use a system, such as Christie's Qualitative Analysis System (QAS), to gain valuable, qualitative information on their students' reading strategies. In the QAS, three questions are answered about each miscue:

- Is the miscue graphically similar at the beginning of the word? In the middle? At the end?
- Is the miscue both semantically acceptable in the context of the preceding text *and* syntactically acceptable?
- Was the miscue independently self-corrected by the student?

Miscue analysis has not been used to any great extent to analyze the reading strategies of students who are blind. However, Sowell and Sledge's (1986) analysis of a student's miscues in braille reading concluded that miscue analysis is a valuable assessment strategy for students who are blind. These authors suggested useful guidelines for judging graphic similarity, which differs in some respects in braille reading and in print reading. Judgments of semantic and syntactic acceptability and self-corrections do not differ in miscue analyses of students who read by braille.

Cloze Procedures

Cloze tests of reading assess a student's use of contextual cues in a reading passage to fill in words that have been omitted. Froese (1991) presented the following directions for the most commonly used cloze procedure:

- Select a reading passage of about 250 words.
- Leave the first sentence intact. Beginning with the second sentence, delete each 5th word and replace it with a blank of equal length. Leave the last sentence intact.
- Instruct the student to read the passage and write words in the blanks that will complete the sentences.
- If the student provides exact replacements for 44% to 57% of the omitted words, the text is at his or her instructional level.

Cloze passages can be used to determine a student's instructional reading level and whether a given set of instructional materials or books are at the appropriate level. This technique can also be used for instructional purposes to foster growth in the use of contextual cues for reading.

When cloze procedures are used with students who are blind, the student may say aloud the words that would fit in the blanks or write answers on a separate sheet of paper. If the student is expected to write answers on a separate sheet of paper, then the teacher should number the blanks when transcribing the cloze passage.

Holistic Scoring

This assessment technique is generally used to judge the quality of a student's writing skills in relation to others in a given classroom, school, or school district; or the teacher may use it to provide feedback to a student on an essay test so he or she will know why a particular score or grade was received (Cockrum & Castillo, 1991). To use holistic scoring, students must first write papers on the same topic, generally in response to a specific writing task, or "prompt." Then the teacher makes a quick judgment about each piece of writing from an overall impression of its quality—guided by examples (called anchors) and criteria describing various degrees of quality (called rubrics)—and rates each paper, generally on a scale of 1 to 5. According to Cockrum & Castillo (1991, p. 83), "It is assumed that this overall impression is influenced by the writer's ability to use the mechanics of language as well as the quality of the content."

A type of holistic scoring is also used to measure cohesion in writing—"the various ways in which writers gather and order ideas" (Mullis & Mellon, 1980, p. 22). To judge cohesion holistically, a rating scale is developed in which each score represents a level of cohesion. For example, 1 may represent little evidence of cohesion, whereas 4 may represent a high level of cohesion that results in a sense of "wholeness" in the writing.

Analytic Scales

Analytic scales are similar to holistic scoring, since they do not involve counting specific errors or features in a student's writing (Cooper, 1977). However, they allow the teacher to identify specific strengths and weaknesses in a student's writing, which is not possible with holistic scoring. Generally, four or more features of writing are identified, and each feature is judged in reference to a high, middle, and low numeric scale. For example, an analytic scale may judge ideas, organization, style, grammar, punctuation, spelling, and penmanship. For each feature, the teacher rates a student's paper from 1 (weak) to 5 (excellent) and then adds the individual scores to derive the total score. If certain features, such as ideas and organization, are considered to be more important than others, they can be assigned higher numbers.

Koenig (1988) developed an analytic scale to assess the legibility of braille writing samples. In his study, competent adult readers of braille were asked to identify essential factors that influence the legibility of braille. Four major categories were identified as important to legibility—braille code usage, correction techniques, formatting techniques, and capitalization/punctuation—from which 11 subcategories emerged. Then descriptors were used to characterize various levels of legibility in the subcategories.

Atomistic Methods

Atomistic methods are used to identify and count specific features of writing or specific errors. Isaacson (1984) identified a variety of such specific features:
- fluency—the number of words in a story or paper
- cohesion—the number of specific cohesive ties in a paper

- conventions—the proportion of correct usage in such areas as spelling, punctuation, handwriting, and grammar
- syntax—the average number of words per independent clause plus any associated dependent clauses
- vocabulary—the proportion of large words, low-frequency words, or unrepeated words.

Among the numerous atomistic measures in writing, almost all are available for judicious use in evaluating writing by braille. A notable exception is "penmanship," although the more general area of legibility is a feature that can be judged in braille writing samples.

ASSESSMENT OF LITERACY FOR STUDENTS WHO ARE BLIND

The Challenge for Meaningful Assessment

Most teachers and parents would agree that changes need to be made in the assessment procedures used with students who are blind. All agree that accurate, reliable, valid, and useful information is needed about a student's literacy development. Such information should be used directly to develop high-quality instructional programs to foster the growth of literacy in students who are blind. To make such changes, however, most teachers and assessment personnel will need to alter dramatically their approach to assessment.

For meaningful progress to be made in the appropriate assessment of students who are blind, the role of norm-referenced, standardized tests must decrease or, as some argue, be eliminated. The results of such tests must be supplemented or replaced by a variety of assessment processes and measures that will provide teachers with the information they need to make good instructional decisions on students and to monitor their progress.

A Framework for Meaningful Assessment

Meaning-centered assessment of literacy for persons who are blind must become a multifaceted, ongoing process that uses authentic procedures for gaining useful information on students. To gain a perspective on the holistic nature of writing assessment in meaning-centered classrooms, it may be helpful to consider Routman's (1991) framework for gathering data on literacy development, which is presented in Figure 7-2. Routman suggested that assessment data should encompass a variety of information from multiple sources and from various learning contexts. The four primary sources, with selected examples, include:

- observation of process—observing reading and writing events within the normal context of the classroom
- observation of product—observing and assessing products created through reading and writing events in the classroom
- contextualized measures—assessments that directly relate to the reading and writing events in the classroom

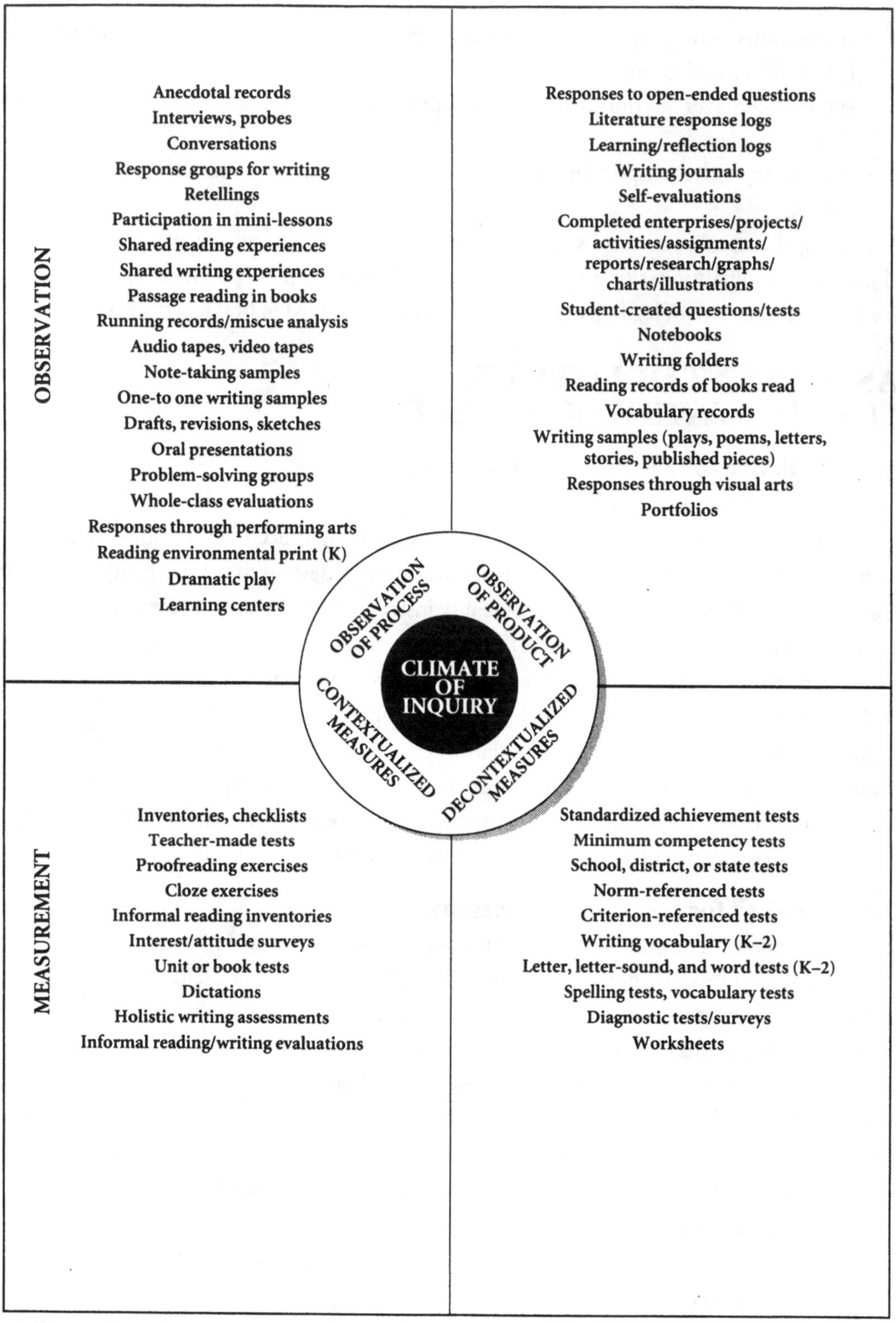

OBSERVATION

Anecdotal records
Interviews, probes
Conversations
Response groups for writing
Retellings
Participation in mini-lessons
Shared reading experiences
Shared writing experiences
Passage reading in books
Running records/miscue analysis
Audio tapes, video tapes
Note-taking samples
One-to one writing samples
Drafts, revisions, sketches
Oral presentations
Problem-solving groups
Whole-class evaluations
Responses through performing arts
Reading environmental print (K)
Dramatic play
Learning centers

Responses to open-ended questions
Literature response logs
Learning/reflection logs
Writing journals
Self-evaluations
Completed enterprises/projects/
activities/assignments/
reports/research/graphs/
charts/illustrations
Student-created questions/tests
Notebooks
Writing folders
Reading records of books read
Vocabulary records
Writing samples (plays, poems, letters,
stories, published pieces)
Responses through visual arts
Portfolios

OBSERVATION OF PROCESS
OBSERVATION OF PRODUCT

CLIMATE OF INQUIRY

CONTEXTUALIZED MEASURES
DECONTEXTUALIZED MEASURES

MEASUREMENT

Inventories, checklists
Teacher-made tests
Proofreading exercises
Cloze exercises
Informal reading inventories
Interest/attitude surveys
Unit or book tests
Dictations
Holistic writing assessments
Informal reading/writing evaluations

Standardized achievement tests
Minimum competency tests
School, district, or state tests
Norm-referenced tests
Criterion-referenced tests
Writing vocabulary (K–2)
Letter, letter-sound, and word tests (K–2)
Spelling tests, vocabulary tests
Diagnostic tests/surveys
Worksheets

Figure 7-2. Evaluation Data-gathering Profile. Source: *Invitations: Changing as Teachers and Learners K-12* (p. 306), by R. Routman, 1991, Portsmouth, NH: Heinemann. Copyright © 1991, Heinemann, a division of Reed Publishing (USA), Inc. Reprinted by permission of Regie Routman.

- decontextualized measures—assessments that are "out of context" or that do not relate specifically to literacy instruction in the classroom, such as state competency tests.

Figure 7-2 presents specific techniques for each of the four elements in Routman's framework.

Although product-centered and decontextualized assessments are included in the framework, Routman warns that "while these are important and valid, we want to be sure that most of the data we are using for informed evaluation comes from observational contexts, especially process" (p. 307). Product-centered and decontextualized information can be useful, *but only as part of a total, holistic view of the assessment process.*

A primary key to meaningful assessment is balance. That is, no single type of measure predominates in the information gathered on a student. One reason why standardized, norm-referenced tests have created such problems for the field of blindness is that rather than considering information from these tests in relation to many other sources of information, the field has focused heavily on this type of data. Changes in assessment procedures may not come easily, but the field must begin to put more balance in the information that is gathered on the literacy learning of students who are blind.

Strategies for Meaningful Assessment

Observation of Process

The process of literacy learning generally is observed when students are engaged in actual reading and writing events. Observations of the process for students who are blind take many forms: anecdotal reports, interviews with students, shared reading and writing experiences, and one-to-one interactions. In addition, videotapes or audiotapes of literacy activities and experiences document students' growth in literacy skills.

Anthony, Johnson, Mickelson, and Preece (1991) suggested two principles to consider when observing literacy learners: (1) observations should occur in authentic contexts and (2) observations should allow the observer to make inferences about what he or she is observing. Data from observations are analyzed through professional interpretation by the observer, who then draws inferences about the implications of the information gathered. For students who are blind, such interpretations should be made by both the special teacher and the regular classroom teacher. The special teacher provides input on the unique aspects of reading and writing in braille, and during literacy conferences, the special teacher, the regular classroom teacher, and the student who is blind collaborate to assess the student's growth in literacy. Without the cooperation of any one of these individuals, the assessment process becomes fragmented and less meaningful.

Observation of Product

Literacy products include sources of data, such as reflection logs on books that have been read, self-evaluations, writing journals, reading and writing portfolios, and writing samples. As is true for students with normal vision, portfolio assessment is an important and valid approach for assessing the growth in literacy of students who are blind; when it is used appropriately, it also prevents the concerns voiced previously with regard to the use of standardized tests. Again, the special teacher and regular classroom teacher should work collaboratively to make the most effective use of portfolio assessment for students who are blind.

Contextualized Measures

This source of data includes the range of measures used or created by teachers for judging growth in the instructional environment. Teacher-made tests and informal checklists are common types of contextualized or classroom measures. In addition, a number of checklists have been developed to assess the acquisition of unique skills related to literacy by students who are blind, including Olson's (1981) comprehensive checklist of behaviors needed in early braille reading and Swallow, Mangold, and Mangold's (1978) various checklists in such areas as braille reading, listening, braille writing, slate and stylus, script writing, and typing.

Teachers who use checklists are encouraged to assess the presence or absence of specific skills in the context of real-life literacy activities. For example, the Typing Skills Assessment (Swallow et al., 1978) asks whether the student can identify the parts of the typewriter, such as the carriage return. Rather than have a student identify the various parts of a typewriter in isolation, the teacher can note during a typing experience whether the student can correctly use the carriage return, for instance. Such an approach ensures that the assessment is truly "contextualized."

Checklists also are available on general literacy behaviors. For example, the Ministry of Education in Victoria, Australia (1990, p. 13) devised "literacy profiles" for elementary students. In the area of reading for the youngest students, a section on "reading strategies" includes the following behaviors:
- locates words, lines, spaces, letters
- refers to letters by name
- locates own name and other familiar words in a short text
- identifies known, familiar words in other contexts.

At the same level, the following behaviors are listed under "what the writer does" (p. 33):
- uses writing implement to make marks on paper
- explains the meaning of marks (a word, sentence, writing, letter)
- copies "words" from signs in immediate environment
- "reads," understands and explains own "writing."

If the special teacher uses such a checklist, it essentially forces him or her to pay attention to higher-level literacy behaviors, rather than to the surface-level unique features of reading and writing by braille. Such a checklist can also provide suggestions for literacy events to be structured for the student, such as making signs and labels accessible in braille throughout the child's environment.

Given the flexibility of informal checklists and inventories, they offer a valuable assessment tool for teachers of students who are blind. Of course, the meaningful use of regular literacy checklists will require meaningful modification, administration, and interpretation. Teachers should also consider chapter tests and other teacher-made tests as valuable sources of information on a student's progress; such information can be collected on a regular basis and summarized when appropriate. Then the teacher will have made a "paper trail" for documenting a student's progress that can be collected in a portfolio and collaboratively evaluated on an ongoing basis.

Decontextualized Measures

Decontextualized measures provide scores from standardized achievement tests, state competency tests, and criterion-referenced inventories. They are called decontextualized because they are not based on learning activities in the classroom. Anthony et al. (1991) did not include standardized measures in this category, since such measures should be used only for program evaluation and similar functions. For teachers of students who are blind, criterion-referenced tests that accompany textbook series and appropriately adapted state competency exams are valuable sources of objective data and are not subject to invalidation as a result of violating standardized procedures.

Concerns over the use of standardized tests were delineated earlier in this chapter. When evaluating the growth of literacy in students who are blind, teachers should use standardized tests only minimally, if at all. When they have a specific need to compare the literacy skills of a student who is blind with students with normal vision, they must include supplementary sources of information or the assessment is not likely to be meaningful.

SUMMARY

The issues surrounding assessment in general are complex and often frustrating. Assessment of literacy is in no way isolated from the more global issues of testing and evaluation. Clearly, all would agree that making assessment more holistic and meaningful will enhance opportunities for it to have a real and meaningful impact on instruction. As Routman (1991, p. 371) concluded, "until meaningful evaluation becomes an integrated part of teaching and learning, tests and decontextualized measures will continue to drive, misinform, and misguide instruction." This statement can serve as both a warning and a challenge.

Professionals in the field of educating students who are blind must endeavor to balance the collection of assessment data among multiple sources of information. They must make the assessment of students' growth in literacy an ongoing activity that occurs in the natural context of learning and living. Above all, they must ensure that their assessment strategies guide their instructional planning and programming so that students who are blind develop appropriate and useful literacy skills.

REFERENCES

Anderson, R. C., Hiebert, E. H., Scott, J. A., & Wilkinson, I. A. G. (1985). *Becoming a nation of readers: The report of the Commission on Reading.* Washington, DC: National Academy of Education, National Institute of Education.

Anthony, R. J., Johnson, T. D., Mickelson, N. I., & Preece, A. (1991). *Evaluating literacy: A perspective for change.* Portsmouth, NH: Heinemann.

Assessing reading in Illinois. (1988). Springfield: Illinois State Board of Education, Department of School Improvement Services.

Calkins, L. M. (1986). *The art of teaching writing.* Portsmouth, NH: Heinemann.

Charney, D. (1984). The validity of using holistic scoring to evaluate writing: A critical overview. *Research in the Teaching of English, 18,* 65-81.

Christie, J. F. (1979). The qualitative analysis system: Updating the IRI. *Reading World, 18,* 393-399.

Cockrum, W., & Castillo, M. (1991). Whole language assessment and evaluation strategies. In B. Harp (Ed.), *Assessment and evaluation in whole language programs* (pp. 73-86). Norwood, MA: Christopher-Gordon.

Cooper, C. R. (1977). Holistic evaluation of writing. In C. R. Cooper & L. Odell (Eds.), *Evaluating writing: Describing, measuring, judging* (pp. 3-31). Urbana, IL: National Council of Teachers of English.

Froese, V. (1991). Assessment: Form and function. In V. Froese (Ed.), *Whole-language: Practice and theory* (pp. 283-311). Boston: Allyn & Bacon.

Gere, A. R., Fairbanks, C., Howes, A., Roop, L., & Schaafsma, D. (1992). *Language and reflection: An integrated approach to teaching English.* New York: Macmillan.

Goodman, Y. M., & Burke, C. L. (1972). *Reading miscue inventory: Procedures for diagnosis and evaluation.* New York: Macmillan.

Harp, B. (1991). Principles of assessment and evaluation in whole language classrooms. In B. Harp (Ed.), *Assessment and evaluation in whole language programs* (pp. 35-50). Norwood, MA: Christopher-Gordon.

Isaacson, S. (1984). Evaluating written expression: Issues of reliability, validity, and instructional utility. *Diagnostique, 9,* 96–116.

Koenig, A. J. (1988). A study of expressive writing skills of blind students including partial replication of the National Assessment of Educational Progress third writing evaluation (Doctoral dissertation, Vanderbilt University, 1987). *Dissertation Abstracts International, 48,* 1734A.

Leu, D. J., & Kinzer, C. K. (1991). *Effective reading instruction, K-8* (2nd ed.). New York: Merrill.

Ministry of Education, Victoria, Australia (1990). *Literacy profiles handbook: Assessing and reporting literacy development.* Brewster, NY: TASA.

Mullis, I. V. S., & Mellon, J. C. (1980). *Guidelines for describing three aspects of writing: Syntax, cohesion, and mechanics.* Princeton, NJ: National Assessment of Educational Progress.

Olson, M. R. (1981). *Guidelines and games for teaching efficient braille reading.* New York: American Foundation for the Blind.

Routman, R. (1991). *Invitations: Changing as teachers and learners K–12.* Portsmouth, NH: Heinemann.

Salvia, J., & Ysseldyke, J. E. (1988). *Assessment in special and remedial education* (4th ed.). Dallas: Houghton Mifflin.

Sampson, M., Van Allen, R., & Sampson, M. B. (1991). *Pathways to literacy.* Fort Worth: Holt, Rinehart, & Winston.

Sowell, V., & Sledge, A. (1986). Miscue analysis of braille readers. *Journal of Visual Impairment & Blindness, 80,* 989-992.

Swallow, R. M., Mangold, S., & Mangold, P. (1978). *Informal assessment of developmental skills for visually handicapped students.* New York: American Foundation for the Blind.

Tierney, R. J., Carter, M. A., & Desai, L. E. (1991). *Portfolio assessment in the reading-writing classroom.* Norwood, MA: Christopher-Gordon.

EPILOGUE

Writing this book has allowed the authors a unique opportunity to review what we know about braille as a medium for literacy. It allowed us to examine critically and, to a great extent, objectively, our instructional and assessment practices. It allowed us time to reflect on the literacy of people who are blind, to let ideas incubate, and finally to come to an unsettling conclusion: relatively little is known about braille as a literacy medium or about the teaching of reading and writing by braille. Therefore, some of the common instructional practices in teaching literacy to children who are blind may not be the best possible practices. The truth is, professionals in the field of blindness simply do not know.

GAPS IN THE KNOWLEDGE BASE

There are many sets of knowledge that guide such disciplines as medicine, agriculture, and education. Those disciplines are based on specific sets of knowledge, such as the teaching of mathematics within education. A "set" of knowledge is often referred to as a knowledge base: a body of wisdom consisting of theory, research, and professional practice.

If a person were preparing for a heart transplant, he or she would seek out a highly qualified surgeon to perform the operation. The surgeon would be recognized by members of that profession as being a qualified professional whose practice was guided by the best and latest research on heart transplants. That is, the surgeon's practice would be grounded in a specialized knowledge base. Should the practice of education be any different? While lives literally may not be on the line in education, *livelihoods* certainly are. When we teach children to read and write by braille, we must do more than just hope that our professional practice is guided by a "body of wisdom." As professionals, we must ensure that literacy instruction for children who are blind is supported by theory and research.

Fundamental research in the areas of braille literacy and reading and writing in braille are summarized in the Selected Research section. However, the authors maintain that the research base in braille literacy, and to a great extent the theoretical base, is fragmented and in dire need of sustained focus. Koenig (1992, p. 283) identified the following gaps in the research base on reading by braille:

- Large-group data on reading achievement and reading rates for students who are functionally blind and use braille as a primary medium for reading are considerably outdated—the last study was in the mid-1960s (see Lowenfeld, Abel, & Hatlen, 1969).
- The efficacy of instructional practices for teaching reading to students with visual impairments, in either print or braille, has not been empirically proven. The exception is *Patterns: The Primary Braille Reading Program* (Caton, Pester, & Braley, 1980), which has undergone extensive field trials.
- The efficacy of teaching reading in braille to students who are *legally blind* has never been empirically established, nor has it been empirically disputed.
- The efficacy of concurrently teaching reading in both braille and print for students with low vision has never been empirically established or disputed.

Similar gaps exist in research on the teaching of writing by braille. For example, we do not know whether use of word processing has a positive impact on writing achievement (although we suspect that the impact is generally positive). Also, there is no research on the best approaches for supporting students who are blind in developing writing skills (or reading skills, for that matter) in whole language classrooms.

Common knowledge, as opposed to true knowledge, is based not on informed and accumulated research, but on "what is always done." It may be that the common practice is in fact the best way to do something, but without a solid knowledge base there is no certainty of the best approach. Consider the following practices in literacy instruction, grounded in common knowledge but open to challenge:

- Students who are blind should begin reading and writing grade 2 braille from the beginning of literacy instruction. *Are there some students who might benefit from instruction in grade 1 braille first?*
- Students with visual impairments should begin reading in one primary literacy medium. *Are there students with low vision who would benefit from learning to read in both print and braille concurrently?*
- Students who are blind need to be of average intelligence to learn to read and write in braille. *Are there students with cognitive disabilities who may benefit from braille literacy instruction for functional purposes?*

In truth, there is wide diversity of opinions among professionals in the field of education for people with visual impairment, and even "common" knowledge is difficult to agree on. The point is that special teachers need a solid knowledge base on which to base professional practices, rather than simply relying on what is commonly done.

NEED FOR RESEARCH

Research on braille literacy is desperately needed, particularly in the following areas:

- *Instructional strategies:* What are appropriate strategies for fostering early literacy growth, teaching basic literacy skills in braille, and teaching additional literacy tools? What are appropriate strategies for teaching braille reading and writing to students with adventitious blindness or with progressive eye conditions?

- *Efficacy studies:* Are current instructional approaches effective? Is teaching braille reading and writing to students with low vision valuable and beneficial? What factors influence success in braille literacy programs?

- *Assessment strategies:* What are appropriate strategies for assessing braille literacy skills and for selecting literacy media? What are appropriate strategies for assessing and teaching functional literacy skills to students with additional disabilities?

- *Large-group studies:* What are the literacy achievement levels and typical reading rates of students who read and write braille? How do the literacy skills of students who are blind compare to students with normal vision? How is braille used in daily life and employment?

Researchers in universities and special research centers (such as the Braille Research Center at the American Printing House for the Blind) cannot alone address the many gaps that exist in the knowledge base—nor should they. Teachers of students who are blind, who engage in the practice of teaching on a daily basis, should consider themselves applied researchers. Swenson's (1988, 1991) articles on supporting the reading and writing process for students who write by braille and Miller's (1985) article on early literacy experiences of her daughter who was blind are excellent examples of research knowledge coming from the grassroots level. If a teacher uses accumulated knowledge and experience only to benefit his or her students and does not share it with others, an important source of practical and useful information is left untapped.

Addressing literacy research needs is a responsibility that must be shared by all professionals in the field through the following levels of involvement in research activities for professionals in the field of blindness and low vision:

- Become an active consumer of research literature.
- Participate in research studies when requested.
- Share successful teaching experiences by publishing experiences in professional journals.
- Conduct joint research projects with an established researcher and publish the results.
- Conduct independent research projects and publish the results.
- Assist colleagues in conducting research and publish the results.

Teachers may justifiably feel uneasy about systematically gathering information on instructional practices and then reporting the findings for publications. Enrolling in an introductory research course at a university will provide an excellent beginning to this exciting dimension of professional practice. Also, pairing up with an experienced writer is a good way to start sharing ideas with the field through journal articles. Former or current university professors may be excited and willing to help in such endeavors. Regardless of role, all professionals can contribute to a rich and extensive knowledge base on literacy for persons who are blind.

TAKING ACTION

Each individual in the field of blindness has a role in improving braille literacy instruction. We hope this book has given you an opportunity to think critically and thoughtfully about the issues that affect the literacy of people who are blind. Professionals can make additional contributions to ensure the provision of quality braille instruction, such as

- Making a presentation at a professional conference or a parent meeting on experiences with a particular literacy instructional approach.
- Volunteering in the community to teach reading and writing to a blind adult who is striving for literacy.
- Becoming part of the Braille Mentorship Project and other literacy activities of the American Foundation for the Blind.
- Becoming part of literacy activities sponsored by consumer organizations, such as the American Council for the Blind, National Association for Parents of the Visually Impaired, and National Federation of the Blind (see Resources section).
- Coordinating activities in the community for Braille Literacy Week, held the first week in January of each year.
- Becoming active in influencing state and national policy that affects literacy for persons who are blind.

The authors hope that each individual who reads this book will take action now to promote and ensure full literacy for all persons who are blind.

REFERENCES

Caton, H. R., Pester E., & Bradley, E. J. (1980). *Patterns: The primary braille reading program.* Louisville, KY: American Printing House for the Blind.

Koenig, A. J. (1992). A framework for understanding the literacy of individuals with visual impairments. *Journal of Visual Impairment & Blindness, 86,* 277-284.

Lowenfeld, B., Abel, G. L., & Hatlen, P. H. (1969). *Blind children learn to read.* Springfield, IL: Charles C Thomas.

Miller, D. D. (1985). Reading comes naturally: A mother and her blind child's experiences. *Journal of Visual Impairment & Blindness, 79,* 1-4.

Swenson, A. M. (1988). Using an integrated literacy curriculum with beginning braille readers. *Journal of Visual Impairment & Blindness, 82,* 336-338.

Swenson, A. M. (1991). A process approach to teaching braille writing at the primary level. *Journal of Visual Impairment & Blindness, 85,* 217-221.

SUGGESTED READINGS

GENERAL LITERACY

Anderson, R. C., Hiebert, E. H., Scott, J. A., & Wilkinson, I. A. G. (1985). *Becoming a nation of readers: The report of the Commission on Reading*. Washington, D.C.: National Academy of Education, National Institute of Education.

Calkins, L. M. (1986). *The art of teaching writing*. Portsmouth, NH: Heinemann.

Goodman, K. S., Smith, E. B., Meredith, R., & Goodman, Y. M. (1987). *Language and thinking in schools: A whole-language curriculum*. (3rd ed.). New York: Richard C. Owen.

Leu, D. J., & Kinzer, C. K. (1991). *Effective reading instruction, K-8* (2nd ed.). New York: Merrill.

Routman, R. (1991). *Invitations: Changing as teachers and learners K-12*. Portsmouth, NH: Heinemann.

Vacca, J. L., Vacca, R. T., & Gove, M. K. (1991). *Reading and learning to read* (2nd ed.). Boston: Little, Brown.

Venezky, R. L., Wagner, D. A., & Ciliberti, B. S. (Eds.). (1990). *Toward defining literacy*. Newark, DE: International Reading Association.

Weaver, C. (1994). *Reading process and practice* (rev. ed.). Portsmouth, NH: Heinemann.

LITERACY AND BLINDNESS

Burns, M. F. (1992). *The Burns braille transcription dictionary*. New York: American Foundation for the Blind.

Edman, P. K. (1992). *Tactile graphics*. New York: American Foundation for the Blind.

Harley, R. K., Truan, M. B., & Sanford, L. D. (1987). *Communication skills for visually impaired learners*. Springfield, IL: Charles C Thomas.

Koenig, A. J. (1992). A framework for understanding the literacy of individuals with visual impairments. *Journal of Visual Impairment & Blindness, 86*, 277-284.

Miller, D. D. (1985). Reading comes naturally: A mother and her blind child's experiences. *Journal of Visual Impairment & Blindness, 79*, 1-4.

Olson, M. R. (1981). *Guidelines and games for teaching efficient braille reading*. New York: American Foundation for the Blind.

Rex, E. J. (Ed.). (1989). Print...Braille...Literacy. [Special issue]. *Journal of Visual Impairment & Blindness, 83*(6).

Spungin, S. J. (n.d.). *Braille literacy: Issues for blind persons, families, professionals, and producers of braille*. New York: American Foundation for the Blind.

Swenson, A. M. (1988). Using an integrated literacy curriculum with beginning braille readers. *Journal of Visual Impairment & Blindness, 82*, 336-338.

Swenson, A. M. (1991). A process approach to teaching braille writing at the primary level. *Journal of Visual Impairment & Blindness, 85*, 217-221.

SELECTED RESEARCH

BRAILLE LITERACY, GENERAL

Mack, C. (1984). How useful is braille? Reports of blind adults. *Journal of Visual Impairment & Blindness, 78,* 311-313.

Conducted telephone interviews to obtain information on how 30 blind adults used braille and their perceptions of the advantages and disadvantages of braille. Found that 97% used braille for noting phone numbers, addresses, and so forth; 17% used braille for pleasure reading; 50% used taped materials for pleasure reading. Also found that the blind adults in this sample used braille "occasionally and/or frequently."

Wittenstein, S. H. (in press). Braille literacy: Pre-service training and teacher attitudes. Report of a national study. *Journal of Visual Impairment & Blindness.*

Used a written survey to examine 1,663 preservice teachers' attitudes toward braille and self-perceptions of competence in braille using a written survey. Found that the majority of teachers had positive attitudes toward braille, appeared confident in their braille skills, and recognized the importance of braille. The type of braille training received (braille code only, braille code plus some teaching methodology, or braille code plus emphasis on teaching methodology) affected attitudes and perceptions of competence.

BRAILLE READING

Ashcroft, S. C. (1960). *Errors in oral reading of braille at elementary grade level.* Unpublished doctoral thesis. University of Illinois.

Studied errors made by 728 blind students in grades 2 through 6 while reading specially prepared braille passages that contained most of the braille contractions and short-form words. Categorized errors in eight categories (from most to least errors for all subjects): missed dots, ending problems, reversals, added dots, association, gross substitutions, up and down alignment, and left and right alignment. Found that short-form words were involved in the most oral reading errors at all grade levels.

Caton, H. R., Pester E., & Bradley, E. J. (1980). *Patterns: The primary braille reading program.* Louisville, KY: American Printing House for the Blind.

Developed a reading program for braille readers—reading readiness through third reader level. Selection of order of vocabulary (including braille contractions), teaching method, and content were based on research in the field. Each level of materials was field tested in variety of settings. Development process prompted additional research, including Caton and Rankin, 1980, and Hamp and Caton, 1984.

Caton, H., & Rankin, E. (1980). Variability in age and experience among blind students using basal reading materials. *Journal of Visual Impairment & Blindness, 74,* 147-149.

> Reader's maturation, experience, interest, and language skills are important variables in selecting materials.

Hamp, E. P., & Caton, H. (1984). A fresh look at the sign system of the braille code. *Journal of Visual Impairment & Blindness, 78,* 210-214.

> Analyzed English braille code as a written code from a linguistic point of view. Provided a set of terms and described a value and meaning for each.

Hampshire, B. (1975). Tactual and visual reading. *New Outlook for the Blind, 69,* 145-154.

> Conducted a study of braille, language, and reading. Reported marked similarity of tactile and visual reading. The only area of divergence was the compatibility between symbols and sensory system used for perceiving symbols. Braille code often interferes with perception of certain language patterns. Results in inability to predict and guess words, possibly accounting for slowness of braille reading rate.

Lowenfeld, B., Abel, G. L., & Hatlen, P. H. (1969). *Blind children learn to read.* Springfield, IL: Charles C Thomas.

> Studied reading rate, reading comprehension, and reading behaviors of 200 fourth- and eighth-grade students who were blind in both local schools and residential schools in the early 1960s. Found that students who were blind were at least equal to students with normal vision and established typical rates for braille reading: 84 words per minute (wpm) in local schools and 72 wpm in residential schools at the fourth grade; 149 wpm and 116 wpm at the eighth grade, respectively.

Mangold, S. S. (1978). Tactile perception and braille letter recognition: Effects of developmental teaching. *Journal of Visual Impairment & Blindness, 72,* 259-266.

> Studied the effects of a developmental program on scrubbing, backtracking, and errors in braille letter recognition with 30 legally blind braille users ranging from 5 to 15 years of age. Used matched samples with experimental and control groups. After completing 227 specially designed worksheets, experimental subjects demonstrated less scrubbing and backtracking behaviors and made fewer braille letter recognition errors than subjects in the control group. The program was effective with both developmental and remedial readers.

Rex, E. J. (1970). A study of basal readers and experimental instructional materials for teaching primary reading in braille. Part I: An analysis of braille features in basal readers. *Education for the Visually Handicapped, 2*(4), 97-197.

> Analyzed four major basal reader series for use of contractions in new vocabulary. Found high percentages of introduction, frequency, and commonality of use. Approximately

90% of single cell-contractions were introduced by end of first grade. Vocabulary control of basal readers appeared to provide an intrinsic control of contractions in braille transliteration. The investigator warned that such control did not take into consideration braille orthographic contingencies such as dual spelling of words.

Rex, E. J. (1971). **A study of basal readers and experimental instructional materials for teaching primary reading in braille. Part II: Instructional materials for teaching reading in braille.** *Education for the Visually Handicapped, 3*(1), 1-6.

Results of the analysis reported in Part I were used to develop instructional materials that addressed braille orthographic contingencies. Materials were programmatic in nature. An experimental group using the materials achieved greater gains compared to a control group following a brief instructional period. Recommendations for judicious use of transliterated texts were made. Related result of the studies was the development of *Patterns*, the specialized braille basal series for blind readers.

Sowell, V., & Sledge, A. (1986). **Miscue analysis of braille readers.** *Journal of Visual Impairment & Blindness, 80*, 989-992.

Used the Reading Miscue Inventory (RMI) to analyze the oral reading miscues of 22 blind students ranging from 6 to 21 years of age. Developed special guidelines for judging the tactual similarity of braille miscues. Found similarities between blind and sighted readers in most areas of analysis, although braille readers successfully corrected fewer miscues (40%) when compared to sighted readers (75-90%). Concluded that the RMI is useful for analyzing oral reading skills of braille readers.

Umsted, R. G. (1972). **Improved braille reading.** *New Outlook for the Blind, 66*(5), 169-177.

High school students were provided with training in accuracy and speed of recognition of each member of the braille code. Training resulted in significant improvement in reading, particularly silent reading. Minimal loss in comprehension occurred with a one-third increase in speed. The investigation used the traditional experimental and control groups and reported quantitative results, but also pointed out the value of its qualitative data, notably that approximately 10 percent of signs were not identified at the pretest level.

Wormsley, D. P. (1981). **Hand movement training in braille reading.** *Journal of Visual Impairment & Blindness, 75*, 327-331.

Trained elementary-aged blind readers to use hands independently. Found that skill in tracking and use of efficient hand movement pattern was closely related to perceptual ability. Younger children learned movement pattern more quickly and with greater efficiency. Recommended combining motor aspects of task with perceptual aspects with beginning reading instruction.

BRAILLE WRITING

Bryant, D. G. (1985). The composing processes of blind writers. (Doctoral dissertation, North Texas State University, 1984). *Dissertation Abstracts International,* 45, 3296A.

> Used composing aloud and other ethnographic methods to examine the composing processes of two adults who were congenitally blind and two adults who were adventitiously blind. Noted differences in planning and structuring the writing task between adults who were congenitally versus adventitiously blinded. Found that subjects who were blind rescanned their writing more than was reported for subjects with normal vision, but concluded that composing processes in these two groups were virtually the same.

Koenig, A. J. (1988). A study of expressive writing skills of blind students including partial replication of the National Assessment of Educational Progress third writing evaluation (Doctoral dissertation, Vanderbilt University, 1987). *Dissertation Abstracts International,* 48, 1734A.

> Studied the expressive writing skills of 29 9 year olds, 33 13 year olds, and 22 17 year olds who used braille. Found that blind 9 and 13 year olds demonstrated comparable or better writing skills when compared to sighted age mates in the NAEP sample on a variety of writing measures; blind 17 year olds demonstrated comparable or slightly weaker writing skills. Concluded that the writing skills of blind children were more similar to, than different from, those of their sighted peers.

Koenig, A. J., & Ashcroft, S. C. (1993). An analysis of errors in braille writing samples. *Journal of Visual Impairment & Blindness,* 87, 12-18.

> Reported another component of the Koenig (1988) study. Coded and categorized all errors in writing samples of blind students. Found that true misspellings were the most common errors and that errors in braille orthography persisted across subjects at the three age levels: 9, 13, and 17 years of age. Also found that most errors occurred in use of lower whole-word signs and contractions governed by variable spacing rules.

Lyenberger-Pfohl, E. M. (1988). A case study of the composing processes of two congenitally blind students. (Doctoral dissertation, Indiana University of Pennsylvania, 1987). *Dissertation Abstracts International,* 48, 3089A-3090A.

> Used ethnographic inquiry to investigate the composing processes in braille of two students in the fifth and seventh grade, respectively, who were blind. Found that both subjects used planning, translating, and reviewing—the basic elements in the writing process. Noted some differences in the subjects' planning and rereading of written work. Concluded that blind students in this study demonstrated similar composing behaviors to students who are sighted.

TACTUAL PERCEPTION

Bliss, J. S., & Crane, H. D. (1969). Tactile perception. *American Foundation for the Blind Research Bulletin, 19,* 269-274.

> Investigations related to memory of the tactual learner. Findings indicate that the three stages of memory of the visual information processing system also operate in tactual information processing system. Findings also suggest a somewhat smaller sensory register and greater decay in both the register and the short-term memory. The ability to "chunk" symbols in working memory functions for blind persons as well as for seeing individuals in the reading process.

Juurmaa, J. (1967). *Ability structure and loss of vision.* New York: American Foundation for the Blind.

> Exemplary study of the ability structure of people who are blind. Studied finger dexterity, tactual discrimination, and kinesthetic mastery of hand positions. Used large groups of blind and partially sighted individuals. Found no significant intergroup differences in tactual discrimination or kinesthetic mastery of hand positions. Found a tendency for people who were totally blind to be inferior on both traits. Findings indicate the supportive role of the visual mode in tactual activities. Age of onset and duration of blindness appeared irrelevant.

Kershman, S. M. (1976). A hierarchy of tasks in the development of tactual discrimination: Part one. *Education of the Visually Handicapped, 13,* 98-106.

> Devised a set of generalizations in the development of tactual discrimination: from large to fine hand movement, early use of active touch to later use of passive touch, and transfer of learning from simple to more complex tasks. A hierarchy of five tasks in tactual development was devised from the generalizations, ranging from tasks involving large solid geometric shapes to braille figures.

Kusajima, T. (1974). *Visual reading and braille reading: An experimental investigation of the physiology and psychology of visual and tactual reading.* (L. L. Clark & Z. S. Jastrembska, Trans.). New York: American Foundation for the Blind.

> Studied finger movements of braille readers. Concluded that visual and tactual reading are identical, with one exception—fixation of the eyes and movement of the fingers. Good readers grouped letters perceptually into words and phrases, not unlike sighted readers.

Nolan, C. Y., & Kederis, C. J. (1969). *Perceptual factors in braille word recognition. Research Series No. 20.* New York: American Foundation for the Blind.

> A series of studies investigating perceptual factors in braille word recognition found that the single braille cell was the perceptual unit of learning. Knowledge now influences

method of and materials for reading instruction. Also found that the ease of recognizing braille characters is affected by factors such as the number and configuration of dots in the cell; recognizing braille words is a sequential integrative process that occurs over a temporal interval; the rate of braille reading skills development appeared to lag behind that for print reading; and mental ability significantly influences braille reading skills development.

RESOURCES

A variety of organizations serve as sources of information and assistance for teachers—as well as parents—of students learning to read and write in braille. Many of these organizations also produce useful publications and supply equipment that facilitates reading and writing by people who are blind or visually impaired in braille or by other methods. This listing contains a sample of such organizations, as well as a number of manufacturers that specialize in equipment for people who are blind. A comprehensive listing, as well as information on organizations and commercial publishers that publish braille books and textbooks, is provided in the American Foundation for the Blind's *Directory of Services for Blind and Visually Impaired Persons in the United States and Canada, 24th edition.*

In addition, as part of its National Initiative on Literacy, the American Foundation for the Blind has undertaken the National Braille Literacy Mentor Project to provide mentors—experienced teachers or braille users—to assist professionals who are responsible for teaching braille to students or adults. Assistance with any aspect of braille instruction can be obtained by calling the National Initiative on Literacy at AFB's field office in Atlanta, Georgia, at (404) 525-2303, or the hotline at AFB's national headquarters in New York at (800) 232-5463.

NATIONAL ORGANIZATIONS

American Council of the Blind
1155 15th Street, N.W., Suite 720
Washington, DC 20005
(202) 467-5081; (800) 424-8666; FAX (202) 467-5085

Promotes the effective participation of blind people in all aspects of society and serves as a national clearinghouse for information. Provides information and referral, legal assistance, advocacy support, scholarships, and advisory services to individuals, organizations, and agencies. Publishes *The Braille Forum.*

American Foundation for the Blind
11 Penn Plaza
New York, NY 10001
(800) 232-5463

Provides a range of services to and acts as an information clearinghouse for people who are blind or visually impaired and their families, professionals, organizations, schools, and corporations. Publishes books, pamphlets, *The Directory of Services for Blind and Visually Impaired Persons in the United States and Canada*, and the *Journal of Visual Impairment & Blindness* and produces videos.

American Printing House for the Blind
1839 Frankfort Avenue
P.O. Box 6085
Louisville, KY 40206-0085
(502) 895-2405; (800) 223-1839; FAX (502) 895-1509

Provides textbooks and educational aids for legally blind students attending elementary and secondary schools or special educational institutions. Produces materials in braille, large print, and on audiocassette; manufactures computer-access equipment, software, and special educational devices for visually impaired persons; maintains a braille research center, an educational research and development program, and a reference-catalog service providing information about volunteer-produced textbooks in accessible media.

Association for Education and Rehabilitation of the Blind and Visually Impaired
206 North Washington Street, Suite 320
Alexandria, VA 22314
(703) 548-1884

Promotes all phases of education and work for people of all ages who are blind or visually impaired. Operates a job exchange and reference information service, provides continuing education programs, and publishes newsletters and a journal. Certifies rehabilitation teachers, orientation and mobility specialists, and classroom teachers.

Braille Authority of North America
c/o American Council of the Blind
1155 15th Street, N.W., Suite 720
Washington, DC 20005
(202) 467-5081

U.S.-Canadian member agencies set standards and strive to promulgate codes regarding the usage of braille and to encourage its use, teaching, and production. Publishes annual directory.

Braille Revival League
c/o Kim Charlson, President
57 Grandview Avenue
Watertown, MA 02172
(617) 926-9198

Promotes braille as the means of literacy for blind people and works to improve availability of braille education. Publishes quarterly *BRL Memorandum*, promotes Braille Literacy Week, and holds an annual conference with the American Council of the Blind.

California Transcribers and Educators of the Visually Handicapped
741 North Vermont Avenue
Los Angeles, CA 90029
(213) 666-2211

Works to establish common transcribing procedures and promote acceptable practices and technology to enhance the education of visually impaired people. Members include transcribers, as well as educators, administrators, parents, rehabilitation counselors, librarians, paraprofessionals, students, and others. Publishes the tri-annual *CTEVH Journal* and *Access*, a guide to resources for visually handicapped persons. Holds an annual conference and free workshops on new techniques and technology, offers low-cost embossing services, and loans low-vision kits to teachers.

Canadian National Institute for the Blind
1931 Bayview Avenue
Toronto, ON M4G 4C8
Canada
(416) 480-7677; FAX (416) 480-7677

Provides a wide variety of rehabilitation and other services, including the operation of a career development center, reference library, and music library.

Council for Exceptional Children
Division for the Visually Handicapped
1920 Association Drive
Reston, VA 22091
(703) 620-3660; FAX (703) 264-9494

Serves as the professional organization for teachers, school administrators, and others concerned with children who require special services. Publishes periodicals, books, and other materials on teaching exceptional children.

Library of Congress National Library Service for the Blind and Physically Handicapped
1291 Taylor Street, N.W.
Washington, DC 20542
(202) 707-5100; (800) 424-8567

Conducts a national program to distribute free reading materials in braille and on recorded disks and cassettes to people who are blind or visually impaired through a network of regional and subregional libraries and machine-lending agencies. Operates a reference information section on all aspects of blindness and other physical disabilities that affect reading and functions as a bibliographic center on reading materials for people with disabilities.

National Association for Parents of the Visually Impaired

P.O. Box 317

Watertown, MA 02272-0317

Provides support to parents and families of children and youths with visual impairments. Operates national clearinghouse for information, education, and referral. Publishes *Awareness* newsletter.

National Association for Visually Handicapped

22 West 21st Street

New York, NY 10010

(212) 889-3141; FAX (212) 727-2951

Produces and distributes large-print reading materials, acts as information clearinghouse and referral center, and sells low-vision devices.

National Braille Association

1290 University Avenue

Rochester, NY 14607

(716) 473-0900; FAX (716) 473-4274

Assists transcribers and narrators in the development and improvement of skills and techniques required for the production of reading materials for individuals who are print handicapped. Provides braille textbooks, music, career, and technical materials at below cost to blind students and professionals and helps meet other braille needs. Provides continuing education to groups and individuals who prepare reading materials for print handicapped individuals through seminars, workshops, consultation, and instruction manuals. Publishes *Tape Recording Manual; Tape Recording Lessons; Guidelines for Administration of Groups Producing Reading Materials for the Visually Handicapped; NBA Bulletin;* reprints and workshops pertaining to all advanced braille codes, tactile graphics, and computer-assisted transcription.

National Braille Press

88 St. Stephen Street

Boston, MA 02115

(617) 266-6160; FAX (617) 437-0456

Provides braille printing services for organizations, including the Library of Congress. Sponsors children's Braille Book-of-the-Month-Club. Sells braille books, including computer manuals, tutorials and reference guides, cookbooks, baby and child care information, Christmas carols, an employment guide, AIDS information, and books on grammar and etiquette. Publishes *Syndicated Columnists Weekly; Our Special;* and *National Braille Press Release.*

National Federation of the Blind
1800 Johnson Street
Baltimore, MD 21230
(410) 659-9314

Strives, with its affiliates in all states and the District of Columbia, to improve social and economic conditions of blind persons, evaluates and assists in establishing programs, and provides public education and scholarships. Publishes *The Braille Monitor* and *Future Reflections* (for parents of blind children).

National Society to Prevent Blindness
500 East Remington Road
Schaumburg, IL 60173
(708) 843-2020; (800) 221-3004; FAX (708) 843-8458

Conducts a program of public and professional education, research, and industrial and community services to prevent blindness through a network of state affiliates. Services include screening, vision testing, and dissemination of information on low-vision devices and clinics.

Recording for the Blind
20 Roszel Road
Princeton, NJ 08540
(609) 452-0606; (800) 221-4792; FAX (609) 987-8116

Lends recorded and computerized textbooks, library services, and other educational resources to people who cannot read standard print because of a visual or other disability. Maintains a lending library of recorded books and acts as a recording service for additional titles.

MANUFACTURERS AND DISTRIBUTORS

American Thermoform Corporation
2311 Travers Avenue
City of Commerce, CA 90040
(213) 723-9021

Manufactures braille embossers; sells braille labels, braille computer paper, and other products.

Blazie Engineering
105 East Jarrettsville Road
Forest Hill, MD 21050
(410) 893-9333; FAX (410) 836-5040

Manufactures braille embosser; paperless braille input/output notetaker with a conventional keyboard that can be used as a computer terminal; braille keyboard and synthetic speech portable notetaker; and other products.

Enabling Technologies Company
3102 S.E. Jay Street
Stuart, FL 34997
(407) 283-4817; FAX (407) 220-2920

Manufactures paperless braille and synthetic speech screen access hardware and software; paperless screen access hardware; optical character reader that converts print into computer file; braille keyboard input device that produces braille-like dots on computer screen for use by sighted transcribers; braille grade 2 translator software; and other products. Distributes other applications programs and hardware.

Howe Press
Perkins School for the Blind
175 North Beacon Street
Watertown, MA 02172-2790
(617) 924-3490; FAX (617)926-2027

Manufactures the Perkins Brailler; standard, large cell, or jumbo dot braille; braille paper; slates; styli; mathematical aids; braille games.

HumanWare, Inc.
6245 King Road
Loomis, CA 95650
(916) 652-7253; (800) 722-3393; FAX (916) 652-7296

Manufactures braille embossers; device to convert braille to typewriter output; electronic braille-writing device that can be connected to a printer and computer keyboard to be used as a notetaker or computer terminal and prints in grade 2 braille or inkprint; a portable electronic communication device that displays both print and braille and can function as a notetaker or computer terminal; braille translation hardware; and other products.

TeleSensory Corporation
455 North Bernardo Avenue
P.O. Box 7455
Mountain View, CA 94043-5274
(415) 960-0920; (800) 227-8418; FAX (415) 969-9064

Manufactures braille embossers; software to convert computer graphics to embossing (requires vision to use); device to convert braille into inkprint; notetaker with a one-cell braille display; device to convert print, handwriting, or computer ASCII text into tactual representation; and other software, hardware, and computer-related products.

INDEX

Academic (basic) literacy, 10-12
Acculturation, standardized tests and, 114
Additional stimulation, principle of, 42
Alphabets, raised-type, 18, 20, 21
America 2000: An Education Strategy, 5, 7-8
American Association of Workers for the Blind (AAWB), 20
American braille, 19, 20, 21
American Printing House (APH) for the Blind, 1, 19-20, 29, 66-67, 107
Americans with Disabilities Act, 1
Analytic scales, 122
Anchors, 122
Anecdotal records, 119
APH Swing Cell, 101-102
Assessment of braille literacy, 1, 111-129
  challenge of, 123
  formal assessment, 111, 112-117
  framework for, 123-125
  informal classroom assessment, 112, 118-123
  meaning-centered, 111, 123-127
  process assessment, 112, 117-118, 125
  standardized literacy tests and, 112-117
  strategies for, 125-127, 133
Association for Education and Rehabilitation of the Blind and Visually Impaired, 20
Assumptive teaching, 73-74
Atomistic methods, 122-123

Background experience (schema), 25-26, 40-44, 62
Barbier, Charles, 17
Bards, blind, 16
Basal reader approach to reading instruction, 64-68, 78, 79
Basic (academic) literacy, 10-12
Battle of the types, 18-20
Becoming a Nation of Readers (Anderson, Hiebert, Scott, & Wilkinson), 64, 111-112
Boston line type, 18
Braille
  adapting standardized tests in, 114, 115
  American, 19, 20, 21
  basic literacy skills in, 10
  British, 19, 20, 21

contractions in, 20, 22, 31, 32, 107-109
conventions in, 50
development of, 17-24
foreign language, 21-22
notetaking devices in, 108-109
perceptual unit in reading, 29
punctuation marks in, 50
reading. *See* Reading; Reading instruction
resistance to, 18
Seven-Line Chart, 23
standard dot, 20
Standard English, 21, 22-24
textbook format, 21-22
uniqueness of, 2-3
writing. *See* Writing; Writing instruction
Braille, Louis, 15, 17, 19, 21, 22
Braille Authority of North America (BANA), 1, 24
Braille Authority of the United Kingdom (BAUK), 24
Braille bills, 66
Braille code(s), 17-24, 30-32, 50
  computer, 21
  inconsistencies of, 31
  intricacy of, 31-32
  music, 21
  Nemeth, 21
  revision and unification of, 1, 20-24
Braille notetakers, 98, 108-109
Braillewriter, 99, 100-102, 103
  Hall, 21
  Perkins, 100
British braille, 19, 20, 21

Cells, braille, 17, 19, 30
Checklists, 119, 126-127
Children
  language development in, 25-26
  language skills of, 6
Children who are blind
  experiences of, 41-42
  language learning by, 2
  teaching of, 3
"Chunking" process, 28-29
Classroom, meaning-centered vs. skills-centered, 84, 93-94
Classroom assessment, informal, 112, 118-123
  analytic scales, 122
  atomistic methods, 122-123
  cloze procedures, 121
  conferences, 119-120

criterion-referenced measures, 120
holistic scoring, 122
miscue analysis, 120-121
observation, 119
portfolio assessment, 118-119
Cloze procedures, 121
Code(s). *See also* Braille codes
  raised-dot, 17-20
  for writing, 49-50
Commission on Uniform Type for the Blind, 20
Communication, 6, 9, 12
  audience-receptive demands, 48-49, 100
  experience and, 41
  Lindemann's triangle, 48
Communication-language integration, 5-6, 43
Community, functional literacy tasks in, 12
Compartmentalization of language arts curriculum, 85
Comprehension framework for reading instruction, 76, 77-78, 80-81
Computer code, 21
Concept development, 25-26
Concept formation, 43-44
Conceptual domain, 43
Concreteness, principle of, 42
Conferences, teacher-student, 119-120
Content area reading instruction, 73-75
Contextual cues, 121
Contextualized measures, 123, 124, 126-127
Contractions, braille, 20, 22, 31, 107-109
Cooperative learning groups, 77
Criterion-referenced measures, 120, 127
Cues
  contextual, 121
  psycholinguistic, 44
Cultural literacy, 8

Decontextualized measures, 124, 125, 127
Descriptive writing, 51
Developmental literacy, 7
Diderot, Denis, 16-17
Directed reading activity (DRA), 64
Discourse, forms of, 51
Discrimination, sensory, 26-27

Drafting, 55, 56-57, 96
Drill and practice software, 95
DRTA (directed reading thinking
    activities), 77

Editing, 55, 56-57, 96
Education of the blind, early
    leaders in, 16-17
Efficacy studies, 133
Electronic mail, 96
Emergent literacy, 9-10, 11, 25-26,
    91
    experiences and, 42
    reading-writing connection and,
        42-43
English Braille, Standard, 21,
    22-24
English language, graphic system
    of, 49
Experience
    of blind children, importance of,
        41-42
    communication and, 41
Expository writing, 51
Expressive writing, 50

Fishburne alphabet, 18
Foreign language braille, 21-22
Fragmentation of language arts
    curriculum, 85
Functional literacy, 8, 10, 12-13

Global literacy, 8
Grade-equivalent scores, 112-113
Guided writing, 92, 94, 108

Hall, Frank, 21
Hall braillewriter, 21
Handwriting skills, 107
Haüy, Valentin, 17
Holistic scoring, 122
Home, functional literacy tasks at,
    12
Howe, Samuel Gridley, 18

Illinois Goal Assessment Programs
    (IGAP), 117-118
Independent writing, 92, 94, 108
Individualization, principle of,
    41-42
Individualized reading, 77
Informal classroom assessment.
    See Classroom assessment,
    informal
Information processing, tactual,
    27-28
Inkprinting, 102
Institute Nationale des Jeunes
    Aveugles, L', 17, 18

Instruction, principle of unified,
    42
Instructional frameworks, 75-81
Instructional strategies, 63, 133
Interactive approach
    to reading instruction, 62, 63
    to writing instruction, 85, 92-93
Interactive software, 95
Interlining, 102

Journal, personal, 52, 92

Keyboarding, 104-107
Keyboards, braille, 98
Kleidograph, 21
Knowledge base, gaps in, 131-132
Knowledge-based literacy, 7-8
K-W-L (know, want, learn), 77

Language. See also Written
    language
    components of, 25
    oral-aural, 6
    redundancy of, 44-45
    visual-tactual, 6
Language arts curriculum,
    compartmentalization and
    fragmentation of, 85
Language arts textbooks, 86-87
Language-communication
    integration, 5-6, 43
Language development, 6, 25,
    42-43
    in the blind, 2, 25-26
    concept development and, 43
    as lifelong process, 38
Language experience activities, 77
Language experience approach to
    reading instruction, 68-69, 96
Language-experience theory, 6
Large-group studies, 133
Learning groups, cooperative, 77
Learning processes of people who
    are blind, 25-33
    for braille code, 30-32
    "chunking" process, 28-29
    language, 2, 25-26
    memory system in tactual
        information processing, 27-28
    movement, 29
    perceptual unit in braille
        reading, 29
    sensory discrimination and
        perception, 26-27
    for visual vs. tactual reading, 30
"Learning to read" vs. "reading to
    learn," 73-74
Lesueur, Francois, 17

Lindemann's communication
    triangle, 48
Listening, 6, 9
Literacy, 1-3, 5-14
    basic (academic), 10-12
    braille as a medium for, 1-3, 10
    conceptual framework of, 6-8
    cultural, 8
    deficit views of, 7
    definitions of, 7
    as developmental process, 5-7,
        38
    early leaders in education of the
        blind, 16-17
    in early societies, 15-16
    emergent. See Emergent literacy
    focus on, 1
    functional, 8, 10, 12-13
    global, 8
    history of, for the blind, 15-24
    as integrated language-
        communication process, 5-6,
        43
    integrated view of, 9
    knowledge-based, 7-8
    levels of proficiency in, 8
    as lifelong developmental
        process, 38
    for persons who are blind, 9-13
    social, 8
Literacy profiles, 126
Literature-based approach to
    reading instruction, 69-70
London, Treaty of (1932), 21
Long-term memory, 28

Mail, electronic, 96
Materials framework for reading
    instruction, 75, 76, 80
Meaning-centered approach to
    reading instruction, 61-62, 63,
    78
Meaning-centered approach to
    writing instruction, 83-85,
    87-92, 93-94
    process in, 90
    purposefulness in, 87-90
    whole language, 91-92
Meaning-centered assessment,
    111, 123-127
Meaning-centered classrooms, 84,
    93-94
Measurement. See Assessment of
    braille literacy
Memory system in tactual
    information processing, 27-28
Metacognition, 45
Methods framework for reading
    instruction, 75-77, 80

Microcomputers, 94-99
  ensuring availability of
    technology, 98-99
  software, 95
  use by teachers, 96-97
  word processing, 95, 97, 106-107
Miscue analysis, 120-121
Moon, William, 18
Moon type, 18
Movement, in learning, 29
Music braille code, 21

Narrative writing, 50-51
National Assessment of
  Educational Progress (NAEP), 8,
  9
Nemeth Code, 21
New York Point, 19-20
Norm-referenced tests. *See*
  Standardized literacy tests
Notetaking devices, portable, 98,
  108-109

Observation
  in classroom assessment, 119
  of process, 123, 124, 125
  of product, 123, 124, 125-126
Oral-aural language, 6

Paradis, Maria Theresa von, 17
*Patterns: The Primary Braille
  Reading Program* (Caton, Pester
  & Bradley), 67-68, 120, 132
*Patterns: The Primary Spelling and
  English Program,* 67
Patterns Library Series, The, 67
Penmanship, 54
Percentile scores, 112-113
Perception, 26-27
Perceptual unit in braille reading,
  29
Percolating, 54
Perkins braillewriter, 100
Persuasive writing, 51
Portable notetaking devices, 98,
  108-109
Portfolio assessment, 118-119
Prewriting, 54, 56-57, 96
Private vs. public writing, 55-56
Process
  in meaning-centered approach
    to writing instruction, 90
  observation of, 123, 124, 125
Process assessment, 112, 117-118
Process writing, 77
Product, observation of, 123, 124,
  125-126
Product writing, 86, 90
Profiles, literacy, 126

Psycholinguistic cues, 44
Psycholinguistic model of reading
  instruction, 61-62
Psycholinguistic process of
  reading, 38, 44-45
Public vs. private writing, 55-56
Publishing, 55, 56, 96
Punctuation marks in braille, 50

Qualitative Analysis System
  (QAS), 121

Raised-dot code, 17-20
Raised-print type, 18, 20, 21
Reading, 35-47
  as constructive, interactive
    process, 38-44
  current view of, 5-6
  IGAP assessment of, 117-118
  individualized, 77
  as lifelong developmental
    process, 7
  miscue analysis of, 120-121
  as psycholinguistic process, 38,
    44-45
  schema theory and, 40-44
  as strategic process, 38, 45-46
  tactual vs. visual, 30
  teachers' roles in, 35-37
Reading instruction, 61-82
  basal reader approaches to, 64-
    68, 78, 79
  comprehension framework for,
    76, 77-78, 80-81
  content area, 73-75
  instructional frameworks for,
    75-81
  interactive models of, 62-63
  language experience approach
    to, 68-69, 96
  for legally blind students, 132
  literature-based approach to,
    69-70
  materials framework for, 75, 76,
    80
  meaning-centered approach to,
    61-62, 63, 78
  methods framework for, 75-77,
    80
  skills-centered models of, 62, 63,
    65
  teachers and effectiveness of, 63
  whole language approach to,
    70-72, 79
Reading-readiness stage. *See*
  Emergent literacy
"Reading to learn," 73-74, 75
Recorded materials, 75
Records, anecdotal, 119

Redundancy of language, 44-45
Reliability of standardized tests,
  114
Research, need for, 132-134
Revised British braille, 20
Revising, 55, 56-57, 96
Rubrics, 122

Schema (background experience),
  25-26, 40-44, 62
Schema theory, 40-44
School, functional literacy tasks in,
  12
Self-activity, principle of, 42
Semantic domain, 43
Semantics, 44-45
Sensory discrimination, 26-27
Sensory register, 27
Shared writing, 91, 94, 108
Short-term (working) memory,
  27-28
Signature writing, 107
Skills-centered approach to
  reading instruction, 62, 63, 65
Skills-centered approach to
  writing instruction, 83-87, 92, 93
Skills-centered classroom, 84, 93
Slate and stylus, 102-104, 105
Social literacy, 8
Societies, literacy in early, 15-16
Software, 95
Speaking, 6, 9
Special-access technology, 97
Special teachers, 93-94, 98-99
Spelling skills, 107-109
SQ3R (surveying, questioning,
  reading, reciting, and reviewing),
  77
Standard dot, 20
Standard English braille, 21, 22-24
Standardized literacy tests, 112-
  117
  criticisms of, 113
  description of, 112-113
  problems in use with blind
    students, 114-117
Stimulation, principle of
  additional, 42
Strategic reading, 38, 45-46
Student-teacher conferences,
  119-120
Studies, large-group, 132, 133
Stylus. *See* slate and stylus.
Symbols, visual, 15-16
Syntax, 44

Tactile Print Investigating
  Commission, 20
Tactual discrimination tasks, 27

Tactual information processing, memory system in, 27-28
Tactual sense, 26
Tactual sensory register, 27
Tactual vs. visual reading, 30
Teacher(s)
  basal reader approach and, 65-66
  conferences of students and, 119-120
  effective reading instruction and, 63
  instructional frameworks and, 75-81
  microcomputer use by, 96-97
  role of, 8, 35-37
  special, 93-94, 98-99
Teacher-made tests, 126
Teaching. *See also* Reading instruction; Writing instruction
  assumptive, 73-74
  as supportive process, 89
Technology. *See also* Microcomputers
  ensuring availability of, 98-99
  special-access, 97
Telecommunications, 96
Tests. *51   152*
Assessment of braille literacy
Textbook format, 21-22
Textbooks, language arts, 86-87
Texts, transliterated, 66
Thermoform patterns, 107
Touch, sense of, 27-28

Types, battle of the, 18-20
Typing, 104-107
Typing Skills Assessment, 126

Unified instruction, principle of, 42
Uniform Type Committee, 20

Validity of standardized tests, 114
Visual sensory register, 27
Visual symbols, 15-16
Visual-tactual language, 6
Visual vs. tactual reading, 30

Wait, William, 21
"War of the dots," 18-20
Whole language approach to reading instruction, 70-72, 79
Whole language approach to writing instruction, 91-92
Whole language theory, 6
Word processing, 95, 97, 106-107
Work, functional literacy tasks at, 12
Working (short-term) memory, 27-28
Writing, 48-57
  codes for, 49-50
  components of, 54, 85
  current view of, 5-6
  definition of, 48-49
  degree of emphasis on, 85-86
  functionality of, 88-89

functions and corresponding forms of, 51-52
  guided, 92, 94, 108
  independent, 92, 94, 108
  process of, 54-57, 96
  process writing, 77
  public vs. private, 55-56
  purposes of, 87
  rhetorical demands of, 53
  shared, 91, 94, 108
  signature, 107
  types of, 50-53
Writing aloud, 91, 94, 108
Writing instruction, 83-110
  APH Swing Cell, 101-102
  areas of unique need, 99-100
  braillewriter, 100-102
  handwriting skills, 107
  interactive approach to, 92-93
  meaning-centered approach to, 84, 87-92, 93-94
  microcomputers in, 94-99
  skills-centered approach to, 84, 85-87, 92, 93
  slate and stylus, 102-104, 105
  spelling skills and braille contractions, 107-109
  typing and keyboarding, 104-107
"Writing to learn," 75
Written language
  development of, 15-16
  early interactions with, 9-10

ABOUT THE AUTHORS

Evelyn J. Rex, Ph.D., is Professor Emeritae in the Department of Specialized Educational Development, College of Education, at Illinois State University in Normal. She has had a long career as an educator and advocate of literacy, teaching both children with unimpaired vision and students with low vision in the Illinois public schools as well as blind students in the laboratory school at Illinois State University. Her doctoral research at Peabody College of Vanderbilt University was a study of the use of basal readers by blind children. Dr. Rex has written numerous articles and has made conference presentations and conducted workshops throughout the United States and Europe. Among her several honors is the first Access Award from the American Foundation for the Blind for "outstanding efforts to improve access to information for blind and visually impaired people."

Alan J. Koenig, Ed.D., is Associate Professor in the College of Education at Texas Tech University in Lubbock, where he coordinates the teacher preparation program in visual impairment. For the past six years, he has been engaged in research on selecting appropriate literacy media for students with visual impairments and on other aspects of literacy. He recently co-authored *Learning Media Assessment of Students with Visual Impairment: A Resource Guide for Teachers* and is one of the authors of *New Programmed Instruction in Braille.* Prior to entering personnel preparation, he taught in itinerant, resource room, and residential school programs in Illinois and Iowa and coordinated statewide services in the outreach program at the Iowa Braille and Sight Saving School. Dr. Koenig is past president of the Division on Visual Handicaps of the Council for Exceptional Children.

Diane P. Wormsley, Ph.D., is Director of the American Foundation for the Blind's National Initiative on Literacy. She began her teaching career at the New York State School for the Blind in Batavia, New York, where she first learned braille and became fascinated with braille reading and writing. Subsequent teaching posts included positions at Narbethong School for Visually Handicapped Children in Queensland, Australia; Illinois State University; and a two-teacher primary international school located in Papua New Guinea.

Robert L. Baker, Ed.D., is Associate Professor in the Department of Specialized Educational Development, College of Education, at Illinois State University in Normal, where he specializes in teaching and research on strategies of literacy instruction. He was awarded Distinguished Foreign Professor status by Liaoning University in the People's Republic of China for his English as a second language instruction and research based on a constructivist theory of literacy.